FOLK MUSIC

FOLK MUSIC

A Bob Dylan Biography
in Seven Songs

Greil Marcus

Illustrations by Max Clarke

Yale

UNIVERSITY PRESS

New Haven and London

Published with assistance from the foundation established in memory of Calvin Chapin of the Class of 1788, Yale College.

Yale University Press books may be purchased in quantity for educational, business, or promotional use. For information, please e-mail sales.press@yale.edu (U.S. office) or sales@yaleup.co.uk (U.K. office).

Designed by Dustin Kilgore and set by Karen Stickler in Source Serif and WTR Gothic Open Shaded. Printed in the United States of America.

Library of Congress Control Number: 2022930711
ISBN 978-0-300-25531-7 (hardcover : alk. paper)
ISBN 978-0-300-27410-3 (paperback)

A catalogue record for this book is available from the British Library.

10 9 8 7 6 5 4 3 2 1

To Cecily and Steve

"Let me do another song," he said to Wilson.
"I'll come back to this."

"No," Wilson said. "Finish up this one.
You'll hang us up on the order, and if I'm not
here to edit, the other cat will get mixed up.
Just do an insert of the last part."

"Let him start from the beginning, man,"
said one of the four friends sitting behind Wilson.

Wilson turned around, looking annoyed.
"Why, man?"

"You don't start telling a story with
Chapter Eight, man," the friend said.

"Oh, man," said Wilson. "What kind of
philosophy is that? We're recording,
not writing a biography."

—Bob Dylan and friends in the studio with the producer Tom Wilson,
recording "I Shall Be Free No. 10" for *Another Side of Bob Dylan*

CONTENTS

FOLK MUSIC

BIOGRAPHY

Bob Dylan was born Robert Allen Zimmerman on May 24, 1941, in Duluth, Minnesota, where U.S. Highway 61 passes through on its way to its beginning at the Canadian border and its end at the Gulf of Mexico. He grew up in the mining town of Hibbing on the Iron Range, where he led high-school bands playing doo-wop and radio hits, and briefly attended the University of Minnesota in Minneapolis, where he was drawn to the Twin Cities milieu of traditional American music, and began to play coffeehouses in Dinkytown, the bohemian outpost just off campus. In late 1960, he left for New York City; by the end of 1961, as one of many voices in Greenwich Village, the center of the folk revival then making its way through the country, he was recording his first album for Columbia Records, and soon after that was taken on by the manager Albert Grossman, as powerful a man as anyone in folk music. By 1965, through visionary songs that even if they were taken from the news were somehow not time-bound—songs about injustice, war, and the meaning of freedom, at first, as with "A Hard Rain's A-Gonna Fall" and

"The Lonesome Death of Hattie Carroll" performed as if by a troubadour, a lone traveler with a guitar, then, with "Bob Dylan's 115th Dream" and "Like a Rolling Stone" performed by a shape-shifting dandy leading a complete rock 'n' roll band—he was a world figure. "He had taken off as a star into the firmament," the Irish folk singer Liam Clancy said to the biographer Howard Sounes of the many drug deaths and suicides among those in the folk world who were left behind. "He was one of us and, suddenly, there he was. [He] was what every one of us probably hoped to be, and [we] realized now that the lightning had struck. It couldn't strike twice." "The poet laureate of rock 'n' roll!" came the announcement at shows forty years later, with stage manager Al Santos's hysterical tone both quoting and parodying a 2002 piece by the *Buffalo News* writer Jeff Miers previewing an upcoming concert: "The *voice* of the promise of the '60s counter-culture. *The guy who forced folk into bed with rock,* who donned makeup in the '70s and disappeared into a haze of substance abuse, who emerged *to find Jay-sus,* who was written off as a has-been by the end of the '80s, and who suddenly shifted gears and released some of the strongest music of his career beginning in the late '90s. *Ladies and gentlemen, Columbia recording artist Bob Dylan!*" In 2010, he performed "The Times They Are A-Changin' " at the White House (and "vanished without a word," Barack Obama later wrote). In 2016 he was awarded the Nobel Prize for literature. In 2020, with the posting of his seventeen-minute "Murder Most Foul" on his own website, he topped the Billboard singles chart for the first time. In the fall of 2021 he announced a tour scheduled to run through 2024. Across the top of the tour poster was a banner. *THINGS AREN'T WHAT THEY WERE* . . . it read.

IN OTHER LIVES

"I can see myself in others," Bob Dylan said in Rome in 2001, speaking to a crowd of journalists, and if there is a key to his work from now back to its start, that may be it. The engine of his songs is empathy: the desire and the ability to enter other lives, even to restage and re-enact the dramas others have played out, in search of different endings. That can mean slipping into a situation—historical, as with the men behind the different voices in "Who Killed Davy Moore?" or invented, as with the farmer in "Ballad of Hollis Brown," or inherited from other songs, especially songs without named authors or knowable provenance, as from the stage if never on record the thief in "When First Unto This Country," or in "Jim Jones" on *Good As I Been to You* in 1992—and inhabiting its character so fully he is living that character's life as you listen. It can mean trying to rescue someone from drowning, as the singer confronts a seduced and abandoned young woman in "Like a Rolling Stone." It can also mean entering alternate lives and identities one has made up, or discovered, for oneself, as in the transformations of costume, face, hairstyle, and affect

Bob Dylan has himself inhabited, as if in a cliff-hanging movie serial of appearance and disappearance, now the next Woody Guthrie, then the last Rimbaud, now the country homesteader, then the preacher damning crowds to hell, now the archivist of what he once called "historical-traditional music," then a highwayman whispering about leaving bodies on the road—and as the filmmaker Todd Haynes puts it, "once one of those people is replaced by another you never see him again." "I once wrote a song about Emmett Till in the first person, pretending I was him," Dylan said in 1964. "Writing a song called 'The Death of Robert Johnson,'" he said in 1962, and you can see him trying to convince whoever might have been listening in the Gaslight Café on any given night that he knew what he was talking about. That because, as he would say of Johnson years later, he was "someone who's telling me where he's been that I haven't, and what it's like there—somebody whose life I can feel," as he had the right to sing as a black boy who was lynched in Mississippi in 1955, he had the right to sing as a blues singer who was poisoned by a jealous husband in Mississippi in 1938, pretending to be him, maybe both at once, maybe singing, to the tune of Johnson's "Terraplane Blues," at first clichéd and sentimental, sentimental because it was clichéd, then maybe not:

I feel so lonesome
You know you can hear me moan
Yes I feel so lonesome
Even you can hear me moan

I can't walk, I can hardly talk
My hands are cut down to the bone

Such a trickster's gallery is an argument that there is no knowable self, not for anyone, which is why Bob Dylan could, at eighty, in a 2021 pandemic film noir, sing his songs as if they were by someone else, could then sing "Just Like Tom Thumb's Blues" as if it were first recorded by Frank Sinatra, or why he can take anyone else's life as his own. That includes all of the characters in all of his songs, whether drawn from the so-called real, like Tom Paine in "As I Went Out One Morning," or snatched out of nothing, like the High Sheriff in "High Water (for Charley Patton)," who for all anyone knows might be the 1920s Mississippi blues champion Charley Patton himself, at the wheel of his own new Buick with his spats on his feet—which calls the whole notion of biography, or even biographical significance, into question. "I've been married a bunch of times," Bob Dylan said in 2001. "I mean, I've never tried to hide that. I just don't advertise my life. I write songs, I play on stage, and I make records. That's it. The rest is not anybody's business." What's left of the idea of biography—and in these pages, an attempt at a biography made up of songs and public gestures—is a format, a frame of reference, a source of life for certain songs, perhaps, or certain songs as a source of their writer's own sense of his own life, but never a key to their meaning. Which is to say that for a song, a biography of its writer or performer is at worst not a key but a prison, a way of limiting what a song

7

can say and where it can go by returning it always to its author, cutting the listener, the person to whom the song is actually addressed, out of the picture. And it's to say that at best, at least with a songwriter, a biography is another kind of song. It needs a repeating pattern, the open, idiosyncratic sense of rhythm known in the blues as country time, as present in Bob Dylan's version of Tony Bennett's "Once Upon a Time" in 2017 as in his own "Like a Rolling Stone" in 1965, under the supposedly different stories it presumes to tell.

BLOWIN' IN THE WIND

1962

Featuring . . . in Person
"Sensational!"
BOB
DYLAN
"Blowing in the Wind"

—Advertisement,
Minnesota State Fair, June 18, 1997

Which didn't mean Bob Dylan was blowing in the wind. It meant that if you'd forgotten who Bob Dylan was, you might remember the song. Even if it was "Blowin'," not "Blowing."

* * *

"Kinda ersatz," said my friend Barry Franklin when we first heard Bob Dylan singing "Blowin' in the Wind." It was on the radio on someone's boat in the middle of San

Francisco Bay in the late summer of 1963. Like anybody else in the country, we'd heard Peter, Paul & Mary's almost-number-one version, but it went right past us. Bob Dylan himself wouldn't have been on Top 40 radio; this would have been KPFA, the Berkeley FM station that played folk music along with pacifist lectures, news coverage of the civil rights movement, and movie reviews by Pauline Kael. This wasn't like the hit. Sung in Dylan's less arranged, more staccato voice, the song stood out, and what stood out for my friend was its obviousness: the way it seemed to have been written less by a particular person than by the times in which, for which, it was made. It seemed too easy—the singer was flattering the listener, taking for granted his or her own like-mindedness: *Of course you're on the right side. Of course you believe Negroes deserve equal rights. Of course you're against war. Of course you want all people to live in peace. There are other people who don't feel as we do*—the *we* the song itself presumed to create—*but somehow, for some reason, they*—a *they* the song created, too, even as it perhaps opened a door—*just don't see.* It was my least favorite track on Bob Dylan's second album, the first of his I ever bought, *The Freewheelin' Bob Dylan*. Sometimes, playing the LP over and over in my dorm room at Berkeley, my Nicaraguan roommate insisting we play a Joan Baez album instead, I'd lift up the tone arm on the phonograph and skip it. That reaction was, maybe, a residue of what Dylan himself had left in the tune: "When I started writing all those songs and everyone started calling me a genius—genius this and genius that," he once told his biographer Robert Shelton. "I knew it was bull, because I still hadn't written what I wanted to. I had written 'Blowin' in the Wind,' but I wasn't satisfied with that. I was never satisfied with 'Blowin' in the Wind.' I wrote that in ten minutes. 'Blowin' in the Wind' was a lucky classic song. No more, no less than 'Your Cheatin' Heart.' But it was one-dimensional."

Many years later, in 2011, I was asked to write an afterword for a children's book of the song—illustrated lyrics by Jon J Muth, with a one-song CD sleeved in the inside cover. I took the job for the money, feeling like a fraud—after all, I didn't even like the song. I didn't think, in some sense, that the song was morally *right,* or anyway thought that it was morally cheap—but as I listened to the song again, it began to open up for me in a way that it never had before. It seemed not obvious but unfinished. Something was unfinished. Maybe the writer had left the song unfinished so that history could finish it. I didn't know. But now the song felt like a small miracle. It still didn't sound as if it was written by a particular person. It sounded like a few sentences I wouldn't come across until twenty years after I first heard "Blowin' in the Wind," from an obscure radical journal published in Paris the same year "Blowin' in the Wind" appeared on the radio: "The moment of real poetry, which has 'all the time in the world before it,' invariably wants to reorient the entire world and the entire future to its own ends. As long as it lasts its demands admit of no compromise. It brings back into play all the unsettled debts of history." Those words rang like a bell for me: the bell that the song, when I first heard it, and dismissed it, and more or less forgot it, didn't ring. But now those sentences rang the bell of the song, and I tried to write down the echoes. They can do as well as anything I have to start off the story I hope to follow:

The words you've just read, the pictures you've looked at—the story they tell—come from a song written almost fifty years ago by a singer named Bob Dylan: a song called "Blowin' in the Wind."

That was probably before your parents were born. Bob Dylan is an old man now. But he is still singing that song. Almost any night, he might be in your town, playing his music. People of all ages—your age, your parents' age, people older than that—are always there to watch and listen.

"Blowin' in the Wind" asks questions. When Bob Dylan wrote the song, everyone believed they knew what the questions were about.

In our country, in the United States, fifty years ago, many Americans were not treated like real Americans. If you had dark skin, many people thought you were not as good as people with white skin. In many parts of the United States, people with dark skin were not allowed to live where they wanted to live. They were not allowed to vote for president. They were not allowed to eat in restaurants. They were not allowed in movie theaters. Their faces were never seen on television. They were not free.

When Bob Dylan sings, "How many roads must a man walk down, before you can call him a man?" he was singing about this America.

The United States is a very different place today. What was true about the way some Americans were treated by other Americans is not true today. But people are still singing "Blowin' in the Wind." People are still listening to it. Why?

You might be saying—"But the song doesn't say anything about people with dark skin. It doesn't say anything about people not being able to live where they want to live."

That's right. That's because Bob Dylan was able to write about one thing in words that could be about many, many other things too. There are people in his song. There are birds. There are mountains. There is the ocean. There is wind. There are questions, and there are answers. Why is the world the way it is? Why is there war, cruelty, and hate? Will this ever change?

So today, whenever people feel that they are not free—

Whenever they feel they are being treated unfairly—

Whenever they know other people only see what they look like, and not who they really are—

They can listen to "Blowin' in the Wind." They can say,

Yes. I am in that song. That song is about me, too.

Bob Dylan didn't talk about the song altogether differently—as a text to be explained—when he announced it at his show at Carnegie Hall on October 26, 1963. By then "Blowin' in the Wind" was being sung all over the world. *The Freewheelin' Bob Dylan* was a hit: number 22 on the Billboard charts, but in certain multiplying corners of the country, on college campuses, in enclaves of dissent and experiment and folk music in Chicago, Philadelphia, New Orleans, Ann Arbor, Madison, Boulder, Seattle, Los Angeles, San Francisco, it was number one. Show business acts of all kinds were putting "Blowin' in the Wind" on their albums to show their bona fides, to say that however phony anything else on their records might be their hearts were in the right place, as if by singing the song they were making a donation to the NAACP—or SNCC, if they were really hip. Like the character Jenny, introduced as one Bobbie Dylan, playing guitar and singing the song naked in a burlesque house in *Forrest Gump*—as a friend said, "It's meant to underscore a point. That she's still a hippie even though she's stripping." Though as Robin Wright performs the song, it comes off as if it's just one more momentarily popular piece of shlock people strip to, the kind of song you don't hear at all because you're there to watch.

As Dylan appeared at Carnegie Hall—he had flown his parents in from Minnesota for the show—"Blowin' in the Wind" had already been recorded by the opera-trained folk singer Odetta, who when Dylan first heard her in a record store in Hibbing led him to trade in his electric guitar for a "flat-top Gibson"; by the Staple Singers, the gospel

quintet led vocally by twenty-four-year-old Mavis Staples
that was seeking an entry into the pop charts; by the sublime Los Angeles songwriter Jackie DeShannon. Most people sang it piously, like a hymn, as if they were trying to
prove their worthiness to it, and none so much as the Bee
Gees, as they were in 1963. Fourteen years later they would
blanket the world with songs from *Saturday Night Fever,*
but in that year they were three dorky guys with crew cuts
and wide Australian accents who performed the song on
TV as if they were lining up to take communion, or force
it on whoever was watching. In the next year it would be
sung by Marianne Faithfull and Sam Cooke and dozens of
others. In 1965 it was a hit in German by Marlene Dietrich,
who sang it with a sly reserve, as if she were back in the
Blue Angel. In 1997, Bob Dylan appeared in Bologna at
the invitation of Pope John Paul II. He sang "Knockin' on
Heaven's Door" and "A Hard Rain's A-Gonna Fall" before
the pope, in his way, sang "Blowin' in the Wind": "A representative of yours has just said on your behalf that the
answer to the questions of your life 'is blowing in the
wind,'" the pope said in the sermon that followed. "It is
true! But not in the wind which blows everything away in
empty whirls, but the wind which is the breath and voice
of the Spirit, a voice that calls and says: 'Come!' You asked
me: How many roads must a man walk down before you
call him a man? I answer you: one! There is only one road
for man and it is Christ, who said: 'I am the way.'" Maybe
one of Mr. Dylan's representatives had informed a member of the pope's retinue that not twenty years before,

in 1979 and 1980, Bob Dylan was crossing the USA delivering sermons that said exactly the same thing: "Jesus Christ," he said in Tucson, "is the Way, the Truth, and the Life."

At Carnegie Hall, Dylan addressed the song as if it were already on the way to such a world stage. "This is called 'Blowin' in the Wind,'" he said to a loud roll of applause. But he wasn't quite ready to sing it. "I want to tell you a story 'bout it," he said. "I want to tell you a story a friend of mine told me about 'Blowin' in the Wind.'

"He went upstate, visiting a—school. Somebody who went to college up there. With a master's degree, studying to be a teacher. And this friend of mine, they were talking, and somehow the song 'Blowin' in the Wind' came up, and this guy who's got a master's degree, going to become a teacher, says, 'I don't understand that song.' He said, 'Well, what don't you understand about it?' He said, 'Well, I didn't understand that "blowin' in the wind" stuff.' And he said, 'Well, what don't you understand about the song?' He said, 'Well, I don't know, I just don't *get it.*' He said, 'Well, we'll take it apart line by line.'

"'"How many roads must a man walk down"'—he said, 'Do you understand that?' He said, 'Yeah, I understand that.'"

There's a murmur of laughter from the crowd.

"He said, 'Well, "How many seas must a white dove sail"—you understand that?' 'Yeah, I understand that.' Say, '"How many times must the cannonballs fly, before they're forever banned"—you understand that?' He say, 'Yeah, I understand that.'

"He said, 'What don't you understand about the song?' He said, 'Well, I don't understand the "blowin' in the wind," what's that got to do with it?' " The crowd laughs out loud. "He said," Dylan went on, homing in on the punch line, " 'Well, "The answer is blowin' in the wind"—it's *in the wind*.' And he says, '*Ohhhhhhhhhhh—*' "

The crowd erupts. "He say," Dylan finishes, " 'I thought, I thought that he made the song, that he said, "The answer is to blow into the wind"—and you'll find the answer.' " The laughter doubles on itself: "I said," Dylan says, " 'This guy is going to be a teacher! He's got a master's degree!' "

"He had an uncanny ability to complicate the obvious and sanctify the banal," Suze Rotolo, Dylan's girlfriend in the early 1960s, wrote in 2008 in her radiant, painful *A Freewheelin' Time: A Memoir of Greenwich Village in the Sixties.* At Carnegie Hall he opened the song with a very stately harmonica, but around the edges of the theme he's exploring the melody, seeking out its corners, as if the music at least is not obvious, as if it still has things to say he hasn't heard. He sings the song as if it's self-evidently important, with vowels harshly lifted, "Before you can *call* him a man," as if to stress that, as Percival Everett, in his 2001 novel *Erasure,* would have a professor named Thelonious Ellison say in a lecture on deconstruction, "A reiteration of the obvious is never wasted on the oblivious." Dylan sings as if the words of the song are already chiseled on a wall. It's not bad. But the lecture to start: I love that "Well, we'll take it apart, line by line."

*   *   *

Mark Spoelstra was a Village singer Bob Dylan often performed with in 1961 and 1962. He told the Dylan biographer Bob Spitz that Dylan first sang the song in early April 1962 at one of the dinners the Greenwich Village folk music maven Mikki Isaacson hosted.* "He sang a song about someone's death, and I wept," she said once of another occasion. "I was just undone by it. He sang it almost as if he was throwing away his lines. He didn't look at anybody, almost as if he was singing for himself, not for the rest of us." There's heart in those words; you believe them. You want to be there as she was; in moments, between the words, you can imagine that you were. Spitz's only mode is sensationalism; in his telling, after Dylan "strummed through an unfinished version of what would become 'Blowin' in the Wind,' " the "group acted as if it had just experienced a divine revelation. Jaws hung open to the floor." Spoelstra abased himself: "Hey," he says in Spitz's version, "I'm not writing any songs that good!" If it happened like that, it would be the sort of event that

---

* "During that time Bob stayed off and on with Micki Isaacson, who had a one-bedroom apartment on a lower floor of 1 Sheridan Square," Suze Rotolo wrote. "I didn't know much about Micki other than that she was always upbeat and welcoming—a Doris Day type. I don't remember if she had a job; she might have had a trust fund. It was as if Micki were running a hostel for folksingers—she became a kind of den mother. It seemed everyone was sleeping on her floor at some time or other, and it didn't bother her if she had a party the guests never left. There were nights when Peter Yarrow, Jack Elliott, Jean Redpath, and Bobby were camped out on her floor."

the few people who were present would become hundreds telling thousands they were, too. Isaacson is alone in her words. Maybe that's why there's room for others in them.

Dylan first sang the song in public on April 16, 1962, at Gerde's Folk City, a Greenwich Village club where, in the milieu of folk music—in the state of mind of folk music, in a certain sense truly a state, its own country—he had already become a name to drop, a magnet for everyone else's ideas, ambitions, resentments, hunger. Curiosity. It wasn't the first time the song had been sung at Gerde's. Maybe unsure about it, maybe wanting to see how it would play, a few days before, backstage at the club, Dylan had taught it to the singer Gil Turner, also the editor of the mimeographed protest-song sheet *Broadside,* who wrote down the words and took it out front as Dylan watched from the wings. Naturally, given the I-was-there mythologies that seemed to spring up around every step Bob Dylan ever took, at least after the fact, that is not the only version. When Dylan appeared on the cover of the last print issue of the *Village Voice,* in 2017, Happy Traum, a member of the folk group Turner led, the New World Singers, said in an interview that after Dylan taught the song to Turner, Turner, in the Gerde's basement, taught it to the rest of the group, which included Dylan's onetime girlfriend Delores Dixon, and they all went up and performed it. And regardless of the facts that Dylan would record the song in July 1962, and that Albert Grossman would take the song to the collegiate folk group the Chad Mitchell Trio not long after, and that the version on their late 1962 album *In Action* (a very movie-actor manly vocal, a sprightly banjo) would be the first released recording of "Blowin' in the Wind," Traum would go on to say that not only were the New World Singers the first to perform "Blowin' in the Wind," they were the first to record it, too.

The occasion was a November 1962 session for performers who had been featured in *Broadside,* now all gathered in the same room. Most of the songs set down came across less as songs inspired by newspaper articles than as unedited newspaper articles themselves, including contributions from Pete Seeger (an unlistenably tangled protest song about a town run by the Ku Klux Klan), Phil Ochs (a protest song about a man who violated the ban on travel to Fidel Castro's Cuba), Peter LaFarge (a protest song against the segregationist governor of Arkansas Orval Faubus), and Mark Spoelstra (a protest song about civil defense signs). There were the Freedom Singers with "Ain't Gonna Let Segregation Turn Me Around," and Dylan too, as Blind Boy Grunt, with "John Brown," an antiwar protest song, "Only a Hobo," "Talkin' Devil," about the Klan, and, with Traum, "I Will Not Go Down Under the Ground (Let Me Die in My Footsteps)," a protest song about fallout shelters. It was all for the album that came out in January 1963, *Broadside Ballads, Vol. 1,* which opened with the New World Singers' "Blowin' in the Wind," featuring a banjo, painfully genteel lead vocals from Traum and Turner, with Dixon on the answer line of each verse—a recording so slick it sounds like a demo for the Peter, Paul & Mary version, something they could have heard and said, *Well, you know, maybe if we roughed it up a bit*—and closed with their "I Can See a New Day," which unfolded over four minutes, and died before the sun came up. That was one side of the world Bob Dylan was living in.

At Gerde's, on April 16, to raise the song himself he lined out the spaces of a verse and a chorus on his harmonica, strumming his guitar behind the leading instrument, setting a tone, setting a stage. The melody was plainly taken from Odetta's almost biblical 1960 performance of "No More Auction Block," a song sung during the Civil War by African American Union soldiers and former slaves escaped to Canada. The melody was a social fact, something none of the Gerde's regulars would have missed; there was nothing in hiding. "Blowin' in the Wind" borrowed authority from that melody; the long opening instrumental passage established the song's own authority, its own suspense. There is a tingle in the moment. There is a hint of the feeling on a tape that somehow was never erased when in Memphis on July 7, 1954—only eight years before by the calendar, but in cultural time, whole eras before—Elvis Presley, Scotty Moore, and Bill Black found their way through a swampy, midnight re-creation of Bill Monroe and His Bluegrass Boys' "Blue Moon of Kentucky," and the producer Sam Phillips shouted from the control booth, *"Fine, fine,* man, hell, that's different!" and the modern age began. That is the feeling; something new is about to begin. Listening back, now, in its moment in time, in that night in New York, it can bring a shudder.

Dylan keeps his voice modest. There's a slight emphasis on the first word, *How,* but after that the song seems to sing itself, to lead the singer through it, as if he hasn't been there before. He's not telling you anything. He's not preaching. He's passing on something that was passed on to him—but in a queer way.

It's unquestionable that "Blowin' in the Wind" takes its wings from "No More Auction Block." But when Dylan himself sang "No More Auction Block," it could almost have been a different song from the one Odetta sang at Carnegie Hall in 1960, without her guitar, accompanied instrumentally only by the bassist Bill Lee, released that same year on *Odetta at Carnegie Hall.* Dylan's own performance of "No More Auction Block" comes down as a recording made at the Gaslight Café in the fall of 1962, well after Dylan first performed, for that matter recorded, "Blowin' in the Wind"—yet the old song is not something that has been picked clean, by Dylan or the dozens of others who sang it, not least Delores Dixon, who often took it to close sets by the New World Singers. It's whole, a body, a physical presence, looming over the singer as well as whoever might be sitting at tables to hear him. Nothing is stressed, overplayed; there are no gestures at historical significance, of self-importance, or for all that gestures toward the embarrassment of a white singer singing a song about slavery as if he had been a slave, or still was.

"Folk music is wide open for good voices," Dylan said, early on in his time in Greenwich Village, speaking of Odetta, implying that good was the last thing anyone was going to call his voice. "Instead of starting at the bottom in

Opera or Show or Jazz they start at the top in folk music."
You can hear that when Odetta sings the song. She sings
slowly, seems almost to stop, insisting that each word in
the song symbolizes a story too vast to really tell. Every
moment is part of a greater drama she is acting out: her
drama, but not only hers. She was born in Alabama in
1930, and grew up in Los Angeles: "I had a teacher who
because I was a big, black young lady, a young girl, she was
going to make me into another Marian Anderson," Odetta
said in 2007, the year before she died. She trained all
through high school. "The classical music I was singing,"
she said, "was a nice experiment. But it had nothing to do
with my life." In 1949, when she was eighteen, she was in
the chorus of a production of *Finian's Rainbow.* "We went
up to San Francisco," she said. "I think we were the last
of the bohemians. Right after that we had the beatniks—
you know, time was a-changing. Same thing, just called
something else. We would finish our play, we'd go to the
joint—and people would sit around playing guitars, and
singing songs. And it felt like *home.*" And that wasn't all it
felt like: it felt like a whole new language, a whole new way
of being in the world: "Folk songs," Odetta said, holding
nothing back, "were the anger, the venom, the hatred of
myself and everybody else, and *everything* else. I could get
my rocks off with those work songs and things, without
having to say, I hate you, and I hate me, and, well—we
can't even do that *now.*" In 2008, after Barack Obama was
elected president of the United States, Odetta was the first
person he named as someone he hoped would sing at his

inaugural. She died less than a month after the election. She was seventy-seven.

No more
Auction block
For me
No more, no more
No more
Auction block
For me
Many
Thousands
Gone

No more
Pint
Of salt
For me
No more, no more
No more
Pint
Of salt
For me
Many
Thousands gone

Odetta drops the word "thousands" down, stepping away from it, as if to gaze at what it signifies, the single word now encompassing American slavery's more than

250 years, and to preserve the memory of the millions who never lived to see the new world. Paul Robeson had recorded the song in 1947 as a great granite monument; Odetta's voice is like a declaration of prophecy, but modest, even anonymous, before it is anything else, surrounded by a ghostly chorus—the Choir of the Master, under the direction of the radiologist and minister Dr. Theodore Stent of Church of the Master in Harlem. They make you feel the dead Odetta is singing for those surrounding her, the song here calling them from their graves as if they've been waiting since slavery for the chance to make themselves heard, and this night, this woman has made it happen. In your mind's eye you can see a dozen women dressed in white, for purity, but also for shrouds, gathering in shadows. It can make you catch your breath. The performance said everything in barely more than two minutes.

In Dylan's performance, a quick, measured strumming from his guitar suspends the song in the circle of its own melody in the moment it begins. Across four minutes the feeling is unearthly, a hum that seems to have been in the air of history: the sound of bodies going back to dust, the hum of thousands of insects bringing people who once lived into the earth, a hum snatched out of that air and forced to hold still. It will be a constant in the performance: Dylan's version of Odetta's chorus, and yet at once less corporeal—Odetta had real people with her; she was real—and more so, because here the dead rise up. Or rather Dylan, not so much telling a story as bearing witness to it, enters the company of the dead. It is the most powerful early manifestation of the quality that defines Dylan's music in its most uncanny moments throughout his life's work, that quality of empathy. "I can see myself in others": here he sees himself in others, but more than that disappears into them. "I don't carry myself the way that Big Joe Williams, Woody Guthrie, Leadbelly and Lightnin' Hopkins have carried themselves," Dylan said in the liner notes to his second album; here he has found the means to let the song carry him that way. "No more driver's lash for me—no more, no more"—the last four words are holding up an impossible weight of suffering and shame, and you hear the lines less as defiance than as wish. Here Dylan is acting out a story that is not over. The fictional character he has created in the performance is still living the story out. History exists only in the future, when the story can be told out loud. As Dylan tells the story, as he lines it out, in one of the deepest performances of his career, it's still a secret—or worse, a fantasy, a fantasy of freedom that will never come to pass. And yet it has the immediacy of a movie: listen now and you can imagine Chiwetel Ejiofor in *12 Years a Slave* or Jamie Foxx in *Django Unchained* singing it as the credits run. Or Steve McQueen or Quentin Tarantino pulling the old Dylan recording off YouTube and letting him do it.

At Gerde's, at the debut, the shape of the song— "Blowin' in the Wind" built on the skeleton of "No More Auction Block"—isn't the same as it would be when Dylan recorded it just short of three months later. This night, certain words and phrases that would later be replaced were still floating in the air of the song. It was missing what would become a third verse. In the studio, certain hobo-speak affectations would creep in, the costuming of a homeless wanderer passing on home truths that would become official, there forever in the sheet music, the true text: that "Yes'n'" to start off the second and third verses, as if the singer had never been to school but knew the light when he saw it. But not this night in April. This night the song was not a text. Carried forward by its ancestral melody, it seemed at once familiar and odd, as if you'd heard it before but couldn't place it. To listen now to something that has become iconic is to listen to something that, as it was sung that night, is not familiar at all.

How many roads must a man walk down
Before he is called a man?
And how many seas must a white dove sail
Before he sleeps in the sand?
And how many times must the cannonballs fly
Before they're forever banned?
The answer, my friend, is blowin' in the wind
The answer is blown in the wind

And how many years must a mountain exist
Before it is washed in the sea?
And how many years can some people exist
Before they're allowed to be free?
And how many times can a man turn his head
And pretend that he just doesn't see?

The answer, my friend, is blowin' in the wind
The answer is blown in the wind

He ends the song with a quick circle of guitar and harmonica. It's hard to understand what song he could have played before, or what he could play to follow it. There is applause. Present in the crowd were those closest to him: Suze Rotolo, Albert Grossman, soon to be his manager, Dave Van Ronk, his Gaslight Café mentor—and perhaps in the imagination of the singer, or, later, in their own, a phantom cohort: Odetta, Paul Robeson, Rosa Parks, Sam Cooke, Dion, Fannie Lou Hamer, Bobby Vee, Elvis Presley, Woody Guthrie, Bob Moses, John Steinbeck, even the Coen brothers and Llewyn Davis.

* * *

I decided to leave and take a chance on New York. First I lived in the Bronx, and that was terrible. But I'd heard about the Village. There was a Greenwich Village girl in Seattle—a little Roumanian Jewess. I got to know her when I left the woods and lived with her when I was sick. She had painted fans and things—I'd never seen anything like that. So finally I came to the Village. I did sewing. Now I run this little store, and I like it, because I always had a sort of an original taste in decorations and things. I make these blouses myself—they're not afraid of having them too bright down here. Another thing is that nobody cares what

you do down here—nobody expects you to cook or go
to church—and you can always talk to interesting people. I tell you, the West is all right, but it's a great relief
to get some place where you can feel a little bit free. I
know all about those great open spaces.
—Edmund Wilson, "The Road to Greenwich Village," 1925

I like the land, the people that are strange in the
West. I like some of the people, don't like some of
the people. Hard, hard people.
—Bob Dylan, 1961

Bob Dylan arrived in New York on January 24, 1961, by
way of folk havens in Chicago and Madison. "It was a whole
community," he said in 1984 of the old folk landscape, "a
whole world that was all hooked up in different towns in
the United States. You could go from here to California and
always have a place to stay, and always play somewhere,
and meet people." "Got out of the car at the George Washington Bridge," as Dylan told the standard story in 2005 in
Martin Scorsese's documentary *No Direction Home.* "Took
a subway to the Village, went to the Café Wha?" It was an
open stage night; he got up and played. "I looked out at
the crowd and I probably asked from the stage, does anybody know where a couple of people could stay tonight?"
Though that wasn't true at all, he told Robert Shelton some
years before. He and a friend came to New York a month
earlier, in December 1960, and set up as Times Square hustlers: "Sometimes we would make one hundred-fifty or two

hundred-fifty a night between us . . . Cats would pick us up and chicks would pick us up." He didn't make his New York debut at the Café Wha? which in the folk world was like saying you went to Exeter before Harvard: "The first places I played were on 44th and 43rd Streets, between Broadway and Eighth Avenue, in any of those bars." Which was like saying you knocked around with carnies all over the Southwest before you went to Harvard. "Bob was born in Duluth, Minnesota," the folk singer and radio host Oscar Brand said on his *Folksong Festival* program on WNYC-AM in New York on October 29, 1961, Dylan's first radio interview, "but you weren't raised in Duluth, were you?" "I was raised in Gallup, New Mexico," Dylan said in a soft, withdrawing voice. "Did you get many songs there?" "Got a lotta cowboy songs there, Indian songs, carnival songs, vaudeville kind of stuff." "Where'd you get your carnival songs from?" "Uh, people in the carnival," Dylan said, as if amused by his own story: *At least I remembered not to say I ran off to join the circus.* "Travel with it," Brand said, "or did you watch the carnival?" "Traveled with it, when I was about, thirteen years old." "For how long?" "All the way up till I was nineteen. Every year, off and on, I joined different carnivals." "Well, I'd like to hear one of the carnival kinds of music you've been singing, and I know you've been doing quite well, and you'll be singing at the Carnegie Chapter Hall, do you want to pick something out?" "Well, I'll pick out a carnival song that I learned, that I *wrote* there. Wanna hear one a them?" And he went into the standard little folk jig "Sally Gal."

There were any number of people there at the Café Wha? and on the folk grapevine willing to take him in: for his first year in New York, Dylan moved between the apartments or houses of various couples, sleeping on their couches, eating their food, reading their libraries. Within weeks, it seems, he'd met nearly everyone on the scene it was possible to meet. In Hibbing, he'd heard Lead Belly records, heard the southern killer, born in 1888, who seemed to know every song sung on any road, and he felt, saw, heard the earth open up. In Minneapolis, he'd fallen for the ballads, the talking blues, the anthems, the songs of right and wrong, the hobo Don Juan japes of Woody Guthrie, and then for the versions of the same language cooked up by Ramblin' Jack Elliott, first among Guthrie's acolytes. Within weeks after his appearance in Greenwich Village, Dylan was playing on stage with Elliott—but within days he was making weekly visits to Guthrie at Greystone Park Psychiatric Hospital in New Jersey, where the Popular Front troubadour, who himself had played with Lead Belly, dead since 1949, was wasting away from Huntington's disease, the student singing Guthrie's own songs to him. There is a stinging shot in Todd Haynes's fractured, seven-leads cut-up fictional biographical Bob Dylan film *I'm Not There,* from 2007, where the Guthrie character is seen immobile on a hospital bed: he looks like an old prizefighter, someone who took too many hits to the head and who can no longer do anything but stare at the ceiling with a bitterness so intense it can make the ceiling stare back. On weekends, Guthrie was allowed to visit his friends Bob and Sid Gleason in East Orange, New Jersey; they'd make a party of it, bringing Guthrie at least a few steps back into the world. Whether he was staying with the Gleasons or with someone else, Dylan would be there, off in a corner with Guthrie, singing his "Song to Woody," coaxing the ruined old man who wasn't fifty yet, as everyone in the room tried to overhear. "Pete Seeger is a singer of folk songs, not a folk singer," the Gleasons quoted Guthrie, who died in 1967 at fifty-five, for years unable to speak, as Anthony Scaduto, Dylan's first biographer, took down the words ten years later. "Jack Elliott is a singer of folk songs. But Bobby Dylan is a folk singer."

"He cut a *swath* through that scene," said the folk singer Sandy Darlington, who was there to see it happen. The poet Joshua Clover said the same thing in different words: "a figure on the order of Picasso or Stein—sui generis, seeming to lift the entire field onto his shoulders with heroic insouciance, able to create the eventual circumstances for his own reception." As Dylan said forty years after the fact: "I knew I was gonna do it better than anyone ever did it."

After a few months in New York, Dylan went back to Minneapolis for a visit; people were shocked. "He was playing at some party or something, he was like a whole different guy," said Dylan's lifelong friend Tony Glover (1939–2019), looking back in 2005, talking in *No Direction Home,* maybe on the Twin Cities' Light Rail, buildings flashing by as he talked. "You know the stories about bluesmen who go to the crossroads and sell their soul to the devil, come back, all of a sudden be able to do stuff, Robert Johnson, Tommy Johnson, that whole mythology. It was one of those kind of deals almost, when he left Minneapolis, he was just one of five or six other guys doing the same thing; when he came back—." The film goes to Dylan, responding with a grin: "That's when I went to the crossroads and made a big deal. You know"—in a conspiratorial whisper—"*shhhhhhooooot.* One night, and then went back to Minneapolis and it was like, where's this guy been? You know: he's been to the *crossroads.*"

As the year went on he played harmonica with performers as disparate as the foot-pounding blues guitarist John Lee Hooker; the blues singers Victoria Spivey and Big Joe Williams, who had first recorded in the twenties; for his album *The Midnight Special,* Harry Belafonte, whose songs Dylan played in Dinkytown before he discovered Woody Guthrie, in 1961 as much a star as anyone on a stage; and the Texas folk singer and, in Dylan's words, in 2004, in his *Chronicles, Volume One,* "double-barrel beautiful" Carolyn Hester, for her first album on Columbia, the biggest and most respected record label in the country, which did not record scruffy-looking boys-of-the-road folk singers, but did record women who, like Aretha Franklin, on the label at the time and lost in a mainstream makeover, might have a nightclub career in their future.

If that was why Hester was on Columbia, she had a different appeal for Bob Dylan: she had known, she had actually played with, Buddy Holly, who Dylan, at seventeen, had seen play in Duluth just days before he was killed in a plane crash near Clear Lake, Iowa, on February 3, 1959, when he was twenty-two. A *New York Times* review of a Dylan performance at Gerde's was so fulsome ("Mr. Dylan is vague about his antecedents and birthplace," Robert Shelton wrote in an irresistibly balanced sentence, "but it matters less where he has been than where he is going, and that would seem to be straight up") that the day it appeared Dylan read the review out from the stage at Gerde's and performed a talking blues about how he'd stayed up all night reading it. Rehearsing at Hester's apartment, he met her producer, John Hammond, a figure of great command and even greater prestige, who as a record man went back as far as Bessie Smith. After the recording session, he asked Dylan to come in and make demos, and then offered him a contract. The twenty-year-old was allowed to sign because, he said, he was an orphan.

The Shelton review and Columbia separated him from everyone else. "He came in waving a piece of paper and yelling . . . with glee. He announced it to everyone in the room," Mikki Isaacson remembered. "He wouldn't let anybody see it, but he was waving something, and he said, 'I got it! I got it!' And we all looked blank and we said, 'What have you got?' and he said, 'A contract with Columbia.' And nobody believed him." Village folk singers might record for Folkways, Vanguard if they had more concept (the Clancy Brothers) or Vogue looks (Richard and Mimi Fariña), but Columbia was a few steps away from signing with the government. "*Everybody* wanted that," Dave Van Ronk once said. "People couldn't admit to themselves that they were that hungry. They turned it into a moral issue. *They had to,* because otherwise they were going to have to take long looks at themselves, and not like what they saw." "Quietly, Bob said: This is the beginning of what I have always known," Suze Rotolo remembered, the two of them alone in his first apartment, on West 4th Street, a block from Washington Square Park. "I am going to be big. He said it calmly and knowingly, and it was true. No bragging, no Look at me, no Ain't I grand." Not that it was an accident, either. If it was destiny, as Dylan would later claim ("Just like Shakespeare was gonna write his plays, the Wright Brothers were gonna invent an airplane, like Edison was gonna invent a telephone, I was put here to do this," he said in 2001), it was manifest destiny: "Much time was spent in front of the mirror trying on one wrinkled article of clothing after another, until it all came together to look as if Bob had just gotten up and thrown something on," Rotolo wrote. "Image meant everything. Folk music was taking hold of a generation and it was important to get it right, including the look—be authentic, be cool, and have something to say."

Like any record man, Hammond heard music when he listened to music, and he also heard money. When Bob Dylan recorded his first album late in 1961, the jazz critic Nat Hentoff was already writing about what he called "the folk industry." The year had already seen Joan Baez's second album reach number 13 on the pop charts—an album that would stay on the charts for 125 weeks. The first album by Peter, Paul & Mary, the frankly commercial folk group put together by Albert Grossman, hit number one—and would chart for the next three years. The Kingston Trio, the Stanford–and–Menlo College guitars-and-banjo combo that had taken the post–Civil War North Carolina murder ballad "Tom Dooley" to number one in 1958—and by introducing an old, buried American voice to a new, postwar suburban America, in a seeming instant changed the paradigm of pop music—had three albums in the top ten and had been on the cover of *Life* magazine, at the time the premier imprimatur of consequence in the USA. That was a horror to Paul Nelson and Jon Pankake, students at the University of Minnesota and the editors of *Little Sandy Review* in Minneapolis. "We are two people who love folk music very much and want to do all we can to help the good in it grow and the bad in it perish," they wrote in the first issue of their 4″ × 7″ mimeographed magazine with a hand-stapled spine; the second issue featured a cartoon of Pankake madly typing away under a sign reading GIVE 'EM HELL. The voice coming out of the little pages was fierce, funny, snarky, messianic, combative, defiant, sarcastic, with biting wit, the editors aware of their own pomposity and absurdity, poking fun at their own purism without surrendering it. "If you sent your child to a summer camp last year, perhaps you made a mistake," they wrote in a review of Harry Belafonte's *Swing Dat Hammer* and the Paul Robeson compatriot Leon Bibb's *Tol' My Captain.* "Maybe this year you should send him down on the chain gang. They have all kinds of facilities: orchestras and choruses by the hundreds," "guitarists and arrangers too numerous to mention," plus "all sorts of wild sound effects—hammers swinging, spikes being driven, whips, grunts, groans, close-harmony yells"—and that was just a warm-up.

Bouncing ahead from John Henry camp, they devoted an entire issue to an attack on the protest song as an easy answer to what they would call "the nightmare of our folk art," and the mission they felt within it: "to find expression through the basic themes in American life, as stated in traditional music, is the finest musical art for Americans." "This new class of naïve idealists-folkniks romanticizing for never-never utopias and too-clever propagandists working for professional Freedom borrows from the sources it knows best," they wrote in "P-FOR-PROTEST": "The Muck Rakers of the 1930s, the television commercial with its asinine jingles, the pep fest, the Sousa march, the football cheer." It was hard to listen to "If I Had a Hammer," or for that matter "The Times They Are A-Changin'," if you happened across that. They quoted Will Rogers for their watchword: "I reckon some folks figure it's a compliment to be called 'broadminded.' Back home, 'broadminded' is just another way of sayin' a feller's too lazy to form an opinion." Still, they were happy to put a cartoon of the president and first lady on the front of their first number of 1961, JFK on guitar, Jackie on banjo, a nod to the short-sleeved-striped-shirt New Frontier spirit that seemed to animate so much of the folk revival: "On our cover this month is an engaging new group called the 1600 Pennsylvania Avenue Ramblers. The Ramblers, who are bringing a fresh new sound to the Washington, D.C., area with their versions of WHITE HOUSE BLUES and FRANKLIN ROOSEVELT'S BACK AGAIN, have not yet been recorded, but they are close enough to the Library of Congress to afford the hope that something might be worked out there." Given the notion that a new president would take up a tune about the last of his predecessors to be assassinated— D. H. Lawrence was singing "White House Blues" with glee in 1915 to entertain friends: "He set our brains jingling," wrote one, "with an American ballad on the murder of President McKinley with words of brutal jocularity sung to an air of lilting sweetness"—this could bring you up short had you come across that old issue of the magazine after November 22, 1963. "Roosevelt's in the White House, he's doing his best," as the North Carolina banjo player Charlie Poole sang in 1926, putting an unredeemable cynicism into the song that it never lost: "McKinley's in the graveyard, he's taking his rest." That was the version Paul Nelson and Jon Pankake knew and loved; that was what they had in mind for JFK and Jackie's repertoire.

They started with three paid subscribers in early 1960, right about the time Dylan—still Bobby Zimmerman and fresh from writing entertainment copy for the *Minnesota Daily,* the campus newspaper—began performing in Dinkytown. Along with celebrations of Jean Ritchie, Lightnin' Hopkins, the New Lost City Ramblers, and Pete Seeger, a joint review of new albums by commercial folk performers including the Gateway Singers, Bud and Travis, the Chad Mitchell Trio, the Limelighters, the Travellers, and the Brothers Four made it clear that the Kingston Trio was at the top of their bottom list. Dylan sought out Pankake, who in his *Chronicles* he would name as "part of the folk police, if not the chief commissioner," and Nelson, who would become a deep friend, hoping they'd write about him, but mainly for their record collections, parts of which made their way into his hands, at least for a time—finally they showed up, the 6-foot-2 Pankake with a table leg in his hand, to get them back.* He reeled over the rare, U.K.-only Ramblin' Jack Elliott albums Pankake played him, over obscure Woody Guthrie songs, and the treasure chest of Harry Smith's 1952 Folkways Records *Anthology of American Folk Music,* a compendium of irresistibly odd and compelling commercially recorded 78s—on Columbia, Victor, Brunswick, Gennett, the Wisconsin blues label Paramount—from the late twenties and early thirties. But he was also listening to what to Nelson and Pankake was the enemy. "I liked the Kingston Trio," Dylan would say forty years later, as if he were hearing the same thing John Hammond would have heard in him. "I could see the picture."

With the distribution and marketing clout of Columbia behind it, *Bob Dylan* initially sold about five thousand copies. If you consider that four hundred people attended Bob

* "He took about twenty or thirty of them," Nelson remembered, "and he had impeccable taste. He took the best. I saw his notebooks, and he would go through one record and always pick the right song from that record to cover. He had an unerring sense of what was the right stuff."

Dylan's bar mitzvah in Hibbing (Abram and Beatty Zimmerman seemingly invited every Jewish person in northern Minnesota, including two of my own wife's aunts), you can get an idea how small a number that was. But as a commercial failure the album was also a rumor, and its commercial obscurity gave the rumor its force. Everybody knew Joan Baez and the Kingston Trio; if you knew Bob Dylan, you knew something other people didn't, something that soon enough everybody had to know. Within a year, a second album could put an adjective in front of the singer's name as if it were already common coin.

On *Bob Dylan*—except for "Song to Woody," a Guthrie-style talking blues, and a Roy Acuff tune the numbers all folk-world commonplaces, stuff you could have heard in coffeehouses from Dinkytown in Minneapolis to North Beach in San Francisco—you can hear why all this happened in "Pretty Peggy-O" and "See That My Grave Is Kept Clean." The first song, "The Bonnie Lass o' Fyvie" in its Scottish origins, is an utter goof, a stumble-and-fall so full of its own delight that the pieties of the folk revival— where every old song was dressed in its provenance like a suit, where one deviated only barely from the song as it was sung by the person from whom you learned it, where the point was to act as if the song made you as anonymous as any of the true folk people who had sung it in the generations before you were born—were shot down as if the person the singer had named himself for wasn't Dylan Thomas but the Dodge City sheriff who was still dispatching bad guys every week on *Gunsmoke*.

As the founding Texas blues singer Blind Lemon Jefferson recorded "See That My Grave Is Kept Clean" in 1928, he started off with a few jaunty picked notes on his guitar that sound like a fanfare from an old-timey string band. Then a faraway, moaning voice takes over—a voice that seems to be addressing itself to no audience, that seems to be singing to itself. It's the sound of someone thinking more than performing.

He keeps up a quick, cantering pace throughout, his simple but irreducibly definite strum telling you that everything in the song is inevitable. That this is a story that was told before you were here to hear it. That to more than barely form a word—and you hear how the words barely escape Jefferson's mouth—would be to betray the song.

It would be to pretend that any meaning could ever be clear, when what the singer is saying is that the truth is always out of reach. In some way, Jefferson's timing says, this is a story that is older than humanity itself—or that if the first people ever to hear the story were still here to tell us about it, they wouldn't be able to remember who they heard it from.

Have you ever / heard a coffin sound
Have you ever / heard a coffin sound
Have you ever / heard a coffin sound

There's just a slight pause between "ever" and "heard," stronger the second time. As Jefferson, helplessly, it seems, draws out the words in the line—*"everrrrrr,"* *"hearrrrrred"*—that stronger pause adds a feeling of suspense, and this is what Jefferson is playing with. It pays off two verses later, when the slight indication of uncertainty turns into pure melodrama—

Have you ever heard the church bell toll
Have you ever heard the church bell toll
Have you ever heard the church bell toll

—and after the last word of each line, after each *toll,* he strikes two slowly reverberating notes—*drummm, drummm*—the precise touch Robbie Robertson would hit on just after Dylan sang "Where the cape of the stage once had flowed" in "Visions of Johanna" on *Blonde on Blonde,* almost forty years after Jefferson made his song, as if it were coded in the language the two songs shared. Like a scholar, or like a student who has just made the kind of intellectual connection that can make you feel that you can see through walls, Robertson was showing you that "Visions of Johanna" was a version of "See That My Grave Is Kept Clean."

Inside the quickened pace of the song there is something slow and burdened—a three-minute funeral march—and that is how young singers in Cambridge, Berkeley, Austin, Philadelphia, Chicago, and New York were singing "See That My Grave Is Kept Clean" in the early sixties. If they had the nerve, maybe they'd even go for that church-bell note—but usually they didn't, because it would sound fake, like a cheap effect, blowing up a point you'd already gotten, as it almost does when Blind Lemon Jefferson does it.

As Dylan begins the song, he places that bet and clears the table with the unexpected, dramatic, scary dip of a bass note—which turns into a swoop, then a rumble. The movement barely repeats a moment later, then invades the music three times more, and every time the music hasn't prepared for it, hasn't dropped a cue, and it throws you off. The tiny riff communicates a harsh and bitter fatalism, but it disappears each time almost before you can register it, leaving behind that feeling of suspense—in this case, the feeling that the song is breathing down your neck.

As Dylan sings, his voice is scraped and braying: frantic, enraged, immediate, *noisy*. Despite the formally measured pace everything feels rushed. He hammers the coffins shut, tolls the bells—but whoever the singer is speaking for takes this personally. *"Another poor boy's underground"*: you feel the singer knew him. It's as if the singer is saying that now, in 1962, with annihilation hanging over both his audience and himself, he and his audience know more about death than Blind Lemon Jefferson did, and maybe they did: forty-one years later, in 2003, in Erroll Morris's film *The Fog of War,* Robert McNamara, President Kennedy's secretary of defense, speaking of the Cuban missile crisis, held up his hand and bent his thumb to his forefinger, until they almost touched, to show how close the specter had come to turning into fact.

Within the strictures of what folk music was supposed to be, of what it was supposed to mean, what Bob

Dylan did to this hallowed song—the Cambridge singer Geoff Muldaur wasn't just going to sing it, he said, someday he was going to go to Texas and find Blind Lemon Jefferson's grave and sweep it off, and eventually he did— was vulgar, disrespectful, ignorant, and vain. But outside of those strictures, in the bigger world where Bob Dylan would soon enough be heard, it was daring, frightening, and exciting, and its defiance of the rules of its time and place was as much an engine of its performance as its defiance of death—and thirty-five years later, in 1997, when Bob Dylan released *Time Out of Mind,* and the first song, "Love Sick," came on, "See That My Grave Is Kept Clean" would be inside of it. Like a ghost, at first—and then like a body.

The month after Bob Dylan performed "Blowin' in the Wind" for the first time at Gerde's Folk City, the song was published in *Broadside;* it would appear in *Sing Out!,* the bible of the folk world, in June—and that would lead to a scandal that nearly killed Dylan's career in its cradle. The day after his 1963 Carnegie Hall concert, *Newsweek* ran a two-column profile: "He popped up out of nowhere, another unknown, unscrubbed face in Greenwich Village, and now, only two years later, he sits in the pantheon of the folk-music movement," it began. It had a scoop: Dylan's true origins in Hibbing, and, quoting Dylan denying it, his birth name—"implying with relish," Suze Rotolo would write, "that the young man whose 'finger was on the pulse of a generation' was a fake. He was just a middle-class kid from the Midwest escaping a nondescript background."

"*Newsweek* wanted to do a cover piece on Bob Dylan and Grossman wouldn't allow Bob Dylan to be interviewed," John Hammond said years later. "So out of complete frustration and sheer rage, he"—the *Newsweek* music editor Hubert Saul, who as was the rule at newsmagazines at the time wrote without a byline—"did his own research then. And found out this whole story on the telephone. They asked a neighbor if they ever heard Bob sing before, and the neighbor said, 'Don't you remember? We heard him at his bar mitzvah.'"

But this was only a warmup for the knife that was about to go in. "Blowin' in the Wind" was a huge hit, *Newsweek* acknowledged: "There is even a rumor circulating that Dylan did not write 'Blowin' in the Wind,' that it was written by a Millburn (N.J.) High student named Lorre Wyatt, who sold it to the singer. Dylan says he did write it and Wyatt denies authorship, but several Millburn students claim they heard the song from Wyatt before Dylan ever sang it." With people all over the country, and especially in New York, eager to see Bob Dylan stripped down to Robert Zimmerman and sent back to the woods, the story exploded.

Little Sandy Review had devoted five pages to *Bob Dylan*— if there was any judgment Bob Dylan took seriously, or was ready to measure himself against, it was in the pages of the little magazine from Minnesota. "We recall Bob as a soft-spoken, rather unprepossessing youngster: he lived then at the Epsilon Alpha Mu fraternity house near campus, was well-groomed and neat in the standard campus costume of slacks, sweater, white oxford sneakers, poplin raincoat, and dark glasses, and sang the standard coffee house songs (two of his best numbers were Josh White's JERRY and Odetta's ANOTHER MAN DONE GONE)," Nelson and Pankake wrote, and then they pulled out all the stops: the album embodied "the most advanced step yet on records to attempt a universal city style of folksinging which will remain true to the folk, yet also true to the city singer." Having declared war on protest music and the so-called topical song movement ("The new breed of boyos, being neither folk nor artists, alas, apparently wouldn't recognize either folk music or folk style if it were walking along beside them in a Peace March"), the magazine found *The Freewheelin' Bob Dylan,* with its "Masters of War" and "A-Hard Rain's A-Gonna Fall," infected almost from start to finish with the hectoring, self-righteous virus that made even the yearning "Girl from the North Country" and "Bob Dylan's Dream" sound false ("That such a creative energy and driving force as Dylan would ever be satisfied with some of the material issued here is a great mystery"). It did call "Blowin' in the Wind" "Dylan's THIS LAND IS YOUR LAND"—"the song should be with us at least as long as the folk revival (and probably a lot longer)"— which made its response to the accusation against Dylan emblematic. By 1963 *Little Sandy Review* was read by thousands; even people who were regularly dismissed in its pages trusted its writers to say exactly what they thought. And if people who had known Bob Dylan from before he was Bob Dylan could have their own trust shaken, there was no one he could count on. "The big question in folk music circles these days: who wrote BLOWIN' IN THE WIND, Bob Dylan or some high school student in New Jersey?" Nelson and Pankake wrote in their leading column in the very next issue.

We don't know the facts. We wish we did so that we could print them. But, regardless of whether Dylan wrote BLOWIN' IN THE WIND or not, this seems like a poor time to cross him off the list as nothing but a fake. If he has been dishonest, he should be criticized for it; responsible folk music commentators should not close their eyes and mumble "a new Yevtushenko" or "he's the spokesman for this generation." (All of us are roughly the same age as Dylan and he is certainly not our spokesman!) But, at the same time (and despite his unfortunate one-way trip up Topical Song Alley, where he has become a tedious and unoriginal preacher instead of an artist), he has done good work, and will do good work again. (Surely, no one is suggesting that he didn't write any of his songs!) A person of Dylan's stature (despite all the false and overblown image-building, fake Guthrie biographies, and artistic calamities like MASTERS OF WAR and WHO KILLED DAVEY MOORE?) is bound to grow tired of the moronic level of achievement possible in the BROADSIDE genre of song. There are indications that this may be happening (LAY DOWN YOUR WEARY TUNE is an example); let us hope so. We like to think that, beneath all that press agent slop, the

real Bob Dylan is a true and talented artist, not wise,
perhaps, but genuine. That is our shaky and tentative
testimonial; we must be counted in Bob's corner.

The same column in the following number featured a
quick acknowledgment of what had proved a scam, quoting an RCA Victor ad in *Show* magazine: "Dig the latest
outrageous folk advertising bit: 'EDDY ARNOLD, the true
American folk sound! Eddie's new album is full of the
"folk" music he sang before he knew there was any other
kind. That's what makes his GREEN, GREEN so special, his
BLOWIN' IN THE WIND so poignant . . . ' Hmmm," Nelson
and Pankake wrote happily, "a new candidate for the WIND
authorship controversy . . . "

By then the story was out. In 1962 Lorre Wyatt joined
the Millburn High singing group—the Millburnaires.
Claiming it as his own, he brought in a song he'd found in
Sing Out!, confident no one else in the group would have
seen something called "Blowin' in the Wind." The Millburnaires performed it for the Thanksgiving school assem-
bly in November. A teacher asked about the song: Wyatt
said he'd sold it for $1,000—and, just to drape himself in a
little people's credibility, that he'd given all the money to
CARE. He got stories about it into the high-school newspaper. He couldn't stop. Taking over as the leader of the
Millburnaires, he led them to record an album, self-released in early 1963 as *A Time to Sing,* with Wyatt's name
on what came out as "Blowing in the Wind"—if, years later,
the Rolling Stones could claim writer's credit for changing

one word of Robert Johnson's "Love in Vain," maybe Wyatt convinced himself that dropping an apostrophe from the song made it his. The album was picked up by Battle Records, under the same corporate umbrella as Riverside, a major folk label, though Battle was anything but, featuring gospel from the Rev. C. L. Franklin and his daughter Aretha, blues from Memphis Slim and John Lee Hooker, going out of business in 1964 with ten LPs of hot-rod and motorcycle sound effects. They put out *A Time to Sing* as *Teen-age Hootenanny* by the Millburnaires '63: nine guys on the cover, all in ties, most in sport jackets, Lorre Wyatt front and center with guitar and a knowing grin. It was clear from the first notes of "Blowing in the Wind"—the first track of an album that also included "Dona Dona," "500 Miles," and "What Have They Done to the Rain," all, like "Blowing in the Wind," now credited to no one—that the Millburnaires were less students of Lead Belly, or even Dave Van Ronk, than the Brothers Four, whose 1960 hit "Greenfields" was a ready-made Richard Pryor white-voice routine with a plinking guitar. "Blowing in the Wind" was speeded up and dotted with background *oo-oo-oo*s. It was gentle. It was so phony that when Wyatt sang "The answer, my friend," you just knew that whatever he was, he wasn't your friend.

And the impersonation, or replacement in advance— for the Millburnaires' "Blowing in the Wind" did appear well before anyone heard Bob Dylan's "Blowin' in the Wind" on a record, or for that matter Peter, Paul & Mary's— didn't stop there. When the song was published in *Sing*

Out!, Dylan had added a statement, starting off as if before becoming a folk singer he'd worked as a scarecrow, then going back into real speech to get a point across: "June 1962—There ain't too much I can say about this song except that the answer is blowing in the wind. It ain't in no book or movie or TV show or discussion group"—a nice touch you couldn't have seen coming. "Man, it's in the wind—and it's blowing in the wind. Too many of these hip people are telling me where the answer is but oh I won't believe that. I still say it's in the wind and just like a restless piece of paper it's got to come down some time . . . But the only trouble is that no one picks up the answer when it comes down so not too many people get to see and know it . . . and then it flies away. I still say that some of the biggest criminals are those who turn their heads away when they see wrong and know it's wrong. I'm only 21 years old and I know that there's been too many wars . . . You people over 21 should know better . . . cause after all, you're older and smarter." On the back of *Teen-age Hootenanny,* set off from the company liner notes, was a box, titled "PURPOSE," signed by Lorre Wyatt: "Did you ever stop and ask yourself why the hate, the greed, the hunger—the fear? And have you found an answer? Folk music asks these questions— and a lot of others. No, they're not 'pretty' questions, but they're the ones that *must be asked.* But we must do more than just ask: we must do something about them. It is our duty to God, to ourselves, and to our fellow man. 'None is so blind as he who will not see.' The biggest criminals are people like you and I, who see things that are wrong and *know* that they're wrong, and yet do nothing about them. How many times can a man turn his head and pretend that he just doesn't see?"* And the story went on, if not blowing in the wind, then surely twisting in it. "When it was later discovered that Dylan and Wyatt might have crossed paths (Dylan had come to New York to visit an ailing Woody Guthrie at Greystone Hospital, where Wyatt frequently entertained patients by playing the guitar and singing)," one could have read more than fifty years after the fact, "the rumor took an even more scandalous turn: Dylan hadn't <u>bought</u> the song; he'd overheard Wyatt play it at Greystone and then <u>stolen</u> it." And as with the story that Elvis Presley once said, "The only thing Negroes can do for me is buy my records and shine my shoes," some people still believe it all. It was an undertow that Bob Dylan never escaped. "Bob is not authentic at all," Joni Mitchell said in 2010. "He's a plagiarist and his name and voice are fake. Everything about Bob is a deception."

In May 1962—a month before Lorre Wyatt found "Blowin' in the Wind" in *Sing Out!*—Dylan took part in a

---

* Wyatt became a professional folk singer, with a long career that reached its height when in 2012, along with Pete Seeger, he released *A More Perfect Union* (Appleseed), an album of environmental protest songs so feeble, the singers reveling in their own powerlessness, as if that proved their piety, that they were able to sign on the singers Steve Earle, Tom Morello, Emmylou Harris, Dar Williams, and Bruce Springsteen, who was pretty great on the sententious "God's Counting on Me . . . God's Counting on You," stepping out of a collection of twenty-one other singers as if he'd just walked into the room, looked around, and figured God was counting on someone to open a window.

WBAI-FM *Broadside Show*, along with the folklorist and self-appointed Village folk-state general secretary Israel Young, Gil Turner, Pete Seeger, and Sis Cunningham, who, like the future murder novelist Jim Thompson, was part of the Communist Party faction in the Oklahoma City Federal Writers Project in the thirties. Dylan had sung two convoluted protest songs, "The Ballad of Donald White," about a man who is sent to prison for theft and on release finds society so unlivable he begs to be sent back, and "The Death of Emmett Till," when Young, the host, took the mike: "Topical songs have been the topic of this program this afternoon, and I'd like Bob Dylan to sing the last song, called 'The Answer is Blowin' in the Wind.' Because I think that this song, while being a topical song, is just filled with poetry, that people of all kinds can enjoy." Dylan clears his throat and sings in a small voice—as if against that introduction he's trying to make himself small. The song seems very simple. Someone coughs in the background. On the second chorus, Seeger, Cunningham, and Turner come in, and over the space of a phantom last verse—as at Gerde's, the last verse is still not there—they hum through it, before again singing the chorus. They're already singing it as if it's a song everyone is talking about, that everyone knows, that in some way was here before they were, and will be there when they're gone, which, for all but one singing that day, has turned out to be true. Dylan recorded the song for his second Columbia album on July 9, in two takes. The first is touching, earnest, very carefully enunciated; bass notes anchor and focus the music. The metaphors seem clumsy but honest, not arty, not contrived—you can believe someone just sat down somewhere to write and one line followed another. The second take will be the version that is released; it's more assured, more grounded, and sung more freely, the words making their own music. "*Banned*" rings its own bell.

It was the first track on *The Freewheelin' Bob Dylan,* released on May 27, 1963. When Albert Grossman took the song to Peter, Paul & Mary, they thought they were looking at a masterpiece and a hit; they rode the melody, their singing plain, and their version entered the charts a month later, on June 29, selling hundreds of thousands of copies straight off, hitting number 2. In August, Columbia released the *Freewheelin'* recording as a single, which predictably went nowhere—real folk music fans bought albums, not singles, which were Top 40 junk. Peter, Paul & Mary's *In the Wind,* with liner notes by Dylan looking back to the first days of the group as if from the distance of half a century, not a year ("It is 'f these times I remember most sadly—/For they're gone—/And they'll not never come again—"), reached number one.

"It was folk music," wrote Suze Rotolo, who with Bob Dylan walked through the snow on Jones Street, just off their apartment on West 4th, on the *Freewheelin'* album cover, "but it was really rock and roll." It was what Peter Stampfel, who early on Dylan named as one of his favorite singers, and who would go on to form the Holy Modal Rounders and the Fugs, heard in 1961, when Dylan spent a week on Stampfel's couch. As a Village folk singer Stampfel felt trapped in a split between the orthodoxy of folk-lore and his own love for rock 'n' roll, to the point that he couldn't even tell people what he liked. He found that split erased when he heard Dylan. "He had the traditional attitude and style down cold," Stampfel says. "But he'd be singing 'Sally Gal,'" the kind of thing people were singing on flatboats on the Missouri in the 1850s, "with a rock 'n' roll attitude and a rock 'n' roll style. His vocal approach had already gone electric."

James Williamson was a founding guitarist in the Stooges in the late sixties. A few years before he was hav-ing trouble at home. His West Point father hates rock 'n' roll; his mother sends him to an Army psychiatrist, who has him hospitalized; when he shows another patient his switchblade, he ends up in the psych ward. He asks his mother to bring him his Bob Dylan albums: "So here I am, and I laid that needle down on *The Times They Are A-Changin',*" the album that would follow *Freewheelin'* in 1964, "and you could just see the horror, and the unset-tling effect that it had on people in there, until eventually they wouldn't let me play it anymore! That sort of made it crystal clear to me about the impact of this guy, and how much that voice and that message would polarize people." The same thing happened everywhere in 1963. If you were at a party or in an apartment with a new friend, as in my dorm room, people were perhaps less than patient with the scratchy voice you weren't sure you liked yourself. Maybe you'd heard Peter, Paul & Mary on the radio with "Don't Think Twice, It's All Right," another song from the

Freewheelin' album, maybe the disc jockey mentioned it was another song by someone named Bob Dylan, maybe somebody mocked you when you said you liked the Peter, Paul & Mary song, because you hadn't heard the real, first version by the person who wrote it.* Now you couldn't listen to anything else, because you heard something in the Bob Dylan version that wasn't there at all when Peter, Paul & Mary sang the song. It was a voice you couldn't fix, couldn't plumb, and couldn't turn away from, that held an allure you probably couldn't explain, though you tried, mainly by playing the album until you wore it out and had to get another one. You were used to your parents telling you to turn it down; you hadn't expected people your own age, people apparently just like you, telling you to turn it off. If you were there when they weren't, you were pulling out those first LPs that seemed to speak a secret language right out loud in public, a language that translated you, not the other way around. As the first song, "Blowin' in the Wind" was only a harbinger on *The Freewheelin' Bob Dylan*: there were no expectations in the world of folk music or the world of rock 'n' roll for songs with the expansiveness,

---

* "I've got to say thank you to Peter, Paul, Mary, who I all knew separately before they ever became a group," Dylan said in 2015, accepting an award from MusiCares, a charitable foundation of the Grammy Awards. "I didn't even think of myself as writing songs for others to sing, but it was starting to happen and it couldn't have happened to, or with, a better group. They took a song of mine that had been recorded before that was buried on one of my albums and turned it into a hit song. Not the way I would have done it—they straightened it out. But since then, hundreds of people have recorded it and I don't think it would have happened if it wasn't for them."

the intellectual ambition, or the moral weight of "A Hard Rain's A-Gonna Fall" and "Masters of War." People were no more prepared for anything as devilish as "Talkin' World War III Blues," as outrageous as "I Shall Be Free," or as finished as "Bob Dylan's Dream," where it seemed that Bob Dylan was some sort of fictional character that someone else named Bob Dylan was singing about.

You can feel, as you listen to *The Freewheelin' Bob Dylan,* that the person on the cover of the album is on top of the world—seeing all around it, kicking up his heels. "Bob Dylan's Dream" might start from just this vantage point— and what the singer sees is his life as it will unfold before him, where everything he thought was priceless will fall through his hands like water. "I dreamed a dream," he says, floating through the melody of the Child ballad "Lord Franklin," but by the second verse all sense of dream is gone. The young men in the song, the singer among them, are ordinary, and their ordinariness makes them real. You're brought into their ordinary adventures, their ordinary talk, their jokes, their bravado, their ordinary right to claim the world as if nobody before them ever lived in it, and with each line, more of what the song describes slips into the past, until by the end nothing remains: the singer is left with no open road, no friends, and no knowledge. At the heart of an album that began with pure promise, riding the wave of what in a year or two would be called and marketed as a youth revolt, a new generation, a new world, the song rejected youth and walked away. "When you say, 'The future for me is already a thing of the past,' " a journalist started to ask Bob Dylan at a press conference in Rome in July 2001—quoting a line from his "Bye and Bye," a song from the then forthcoming album *"Love and Theft,"* which the assembled journalists had just heard, a line that echoed back to "Bob Dylan's Dream"—but Dylan cut him off. "I say that for everyone," he said. "I'm a spokesman for my generation. I say that for us all." At his next show, in Naples two nights later, he closed the night with "Blowin' in the Wind." "There are certain songs that I will always be able to do," he had said almost a quarter-century before. "They will always have as much meaning, if not more so, as time goes on," thirty-nine years before he recorded "As Time Goes By." There are no straight lines in the language songs speak.

*   *   *

Bob Dylan had become big: recounting the night of that Carnegie Hall concert in 1963, Suze Rotolo, who died in 2011 at sixty-seven, captured the moment as no one else could. "During the concert," she wrote, "the audience hung on every word Bob spoke and sang, and when it was over they gave him a raucous standing ovation. Backstage with Albert Grossman, Dave Van Ronk, Terri Thal, and others, I watched and absorbed what was happening. We all sensed a sea change and it was exhilarating."

At the end of the concert, there was a huge mob waiting for Bob at the stage door, and Albert was concerned that he get into the rented limo in one piece.

Acting as decoys, Terri and I diverted some of the fans by walking in the opposite direction, while Bob and the others jumped into the waiting limo. Those in the crowd who hadn't fallen for the ruse got to the limo just as Bob was sliding into it. Terri and I ducked around the cars to circle back, and as the crowd surged around us we clambered in the door Albert held open.

I remember being very frightened by the energy of the crowd. They literally charged the limousine, pounding on the roof and slapping at the windows, yelling to get Bob's attention. He gave a few staccato waves and then turned away.

As the car slowly moved out into traffic, we gradually lost the fans, who ran behind us. Albert had a Mona Lisa smile on his face. We were all pretty quiet, except for the odd quip, because it was both exciting and scary. Bob was in the right place at the right time with the right stuff. This truly was the beginning of his future: Bobby had become Dylan.

There's a moment to match Rotolo's scene in *I'm Not There:* as Cate Blanchett's Dylan squeezes through the pack of fans into the limousine, a woman, staring straight at him, lights her hair on fire.*

---

* There was a story, at the time, in 1965, that such a thing actually happened. If there was, Todd Haynes says, he never heard about it; as far as he knows, he made the scene up.

*   *   *

"Blowin' in the Wind" lived its own life as if it were a person; it made its own biography. As a folk song, it came from the deepest caverns of the nineteenth century, after the Civil War, when to say, as tens and then hundreds and then thousands of singers did, "a man ain't nothing but a man" was to say he was a man: "If you sang 'John Henry' as many times as me—'John Henry was a steel-driving man / Died with a hammer in his hand / John Henry said a man ain't nothin' but a man / Before I let that steam drill drive me down / I'll die with that hammer in my hand'—if you had sung that song as many times as I did," Dylan said on February 6, 2015, on receiving a lifetime achievement award from the MusiCares charity in Los Angeles, in an extraordinary account of his life as a songwriter, "you'd have written 'How many roads must a man walk down?' too." From the twentieth century it had come out of a family of question-mark protest numbers, from the 1931 Harlan County mine workers' strike chant "Which Side Are You On?" to Pete Seeger's simpering "Where Have All the Flowers Gone?" which the Kingston Trio made indelible anyway in 1961. As a pop hit "Blowin' in the Wind" found its way into "As Tears Go By," the song Mick Jagger and Keith Richards wrote for Marianne Faithfull, Jackie DeShannon's "What the World Needs Now Is Love," and John Denver's "Leaving on a Jet Plane," which in the hands of Peter, Paul & Mary became their only number one hit. "In the early 1960s, folksinger Ian Tyson was sitting in a bar called the Kettle of Fish," just upstairs from the Gaslight Café, the reporter John Mackie wrote in 2017. "A 'kind of grubby kid' walked in and announced he had a new song. 'It was Bobby Dylan,'" Mackie quoted Tyson, "'and he sang me, Blowin' in the Wind . . . He just wrote it. I thought, "I can do that."'" Tyson went home and wrote his first song, "Four Strong Winds"—or, as the 1963 version by Ian and Sylvia would be called years down the line, the unofficial Canadian national anthem. "A folk song has over a thousand faces and you must meet them all if you want to play this stuff," Dylan would write in 2004. "Blowin' in the Wind" had to long outlast its apparent time and place, to go on to where the civil rights movement was barely remembered, to find how many faces it could carry.

So many people have covered the song, to this day, and will next year and in the decade after, that the song fades into a gesture, a wave, performers lining up to get their passports stamped by history. It only rarely sounded not obvious but unlikely. It did sound that way when Elvis Presley took it up at his house in Bel Air in 1966, friends sitting around as he picked his way through the song very slowly, in a heavy, deep voice, slipping the words here and there, repeating words as if to grab the song as it was floating away from him—"and pretend that he just doesn't see— *see*." It feels like a gospel song that he barely remembers. These are just words; he's forgotten what they mean. If he sings them with enough patience, they'll tell him.

It's Bob Dylan who has really investigated the song as

if it were odd. "A few skeptics have suggested that his protest songs of that period ('Masters of War,' 'With God on
Your Side,' 'Blowin' in the Wind') were trendy, marketable
tunes written in cold blood to feed the anti-war, pro–civil
rights sentiments of the 1960s," Neil Hickey wrote in 1975
in a singularly incisive profile. "Not true," Dylan insisted:
"I wrote them because that's what I was in the middle of.
It swept me up. 'Blowin' in the Wind' holds up. I *felt* that
song. Whenever Joan and I do it, it really is just like an old
folk song to me. It never occurs to me that I'm the person
who wrote it." "Where it all began," Joan Baez murmured
a year later when she and Dylan took the stage together for
the tune, in Fort Collins, Colorado, in 1976, near the end
of Dylan's Rolling Thunder tour, Baez in a red head scarf,
Dylan in a white Arab headdress, both carrying acoustic
guitars, and you could see that happen. In an instant, both
the original melody of the song and its source were dissolved in a stop-time, jump-step rhythm, each line a sepa-
rate still image, with Baez putting a lift, a slight harmony, a
sophisticated move, at the end of each verse, letting it float
in the song. "Joan Baez means more to me than a hundred
of these singers around today," Dylan said to Hickey. "She's
more powerful . . . She always did it and always will." You
could see that happen, too, in their faces: her subtlety, his
respect. It's as if, ages back, they took part in a marriage of
affinities: no ceremony, just eyes meeting. The kind where
you can't get divorced.

The same sense of authorless authority was there
almost a decade earlier, up around Woodstock, where,

coming off a world tour in 1966, in 1967 Dylan and his bandmates Rick Danko, Richard Manuel, Garth Hudson, Robbie Robertson, deep into their daily afternoons in the basement of the ugly frame house they were calling Big Pink, found their way out of old Lead Belly songs and into old Bob Dylan songs. "Blowin' in the Wind" unwound as a stripper blues: you can almost see the blue spot on a tired woman going through her motions and the band going through theirs. There is a lot of cheesy organ music. It's just a standard, "Georgia," "Tennessee Waltz," "Blowin' in the Wind," something the combo at Déjà Vu Showgirls on Washington Avenue North in Minneapolis ("100S OF BEAUTIFUL GIRLS AND THREE UGLY ONES" reads the marquee) play to get through the set, the point is to play something everybody knows and nobody's going to question, eyes on the clock at the back of the room, six and a half minutes until break, the singer groaning his way through the number as if he really doesn't know the answers to the questions but, somehow, wouldn't mind finding out. The pace doesn't quicken but the body of the song does: they want to go out big, so they're putting more into it than they would have two minutes before: a sweet, waltzing organ solo, a harsh, probing guitar solo, and as they come back to the last verse it's as if they've stumbled into a big-sky cowboy ballad: "How many times / Can a man look up / Before he can see, see the sky" drops right in. You realize that there's some core of unknowingness, Adam and Eve in the Garden before the apple, or the pockets of folk-song America, the real thing, Black Dog Holler in Kentucky or Jane Alley in New Orleans, where people never learned to read, that makes the song unreadable, which means anyone can do anything they want with it and maybe find a song no one else had ever heard. But the bell rings, the stripper goes backstage, and the guys hit the bar.

In 1985 the great pop music cause was relief of the horrific famine that had begun its ruin of Ethiopia two years before. In 1984 Bob Geldof of the Boomtown Rats enlisted an elite cast of British and Irish performers—at the top, Bono, Phil Collins, and all of Duran Duran—named them Band Aid, and recorded the charity single "Do They Know It's Christmas?" It was a weirdly colonialist title—*Do the benighted wog masses even have the strength to celebrate the birth of our Lord?*—but never mind: it was for the moment the best-selling single in the history of the British charts and raised millions of dollars. Not wanting to be left behind, in January 1985 Michael Jackson and Lionel Ritchie came up with a tune and assembled a similarly celebrated group as USA for Africa—Bruce Springsteen, Stevie Wonder, Ray Charles, Cyndi Lauper, Diana Ross, Billy Joel, Tina Turner—though not the most important performers of their day, Prince, who hated the song, and Madonna, who had tour dates she wouldn't cancel—for the similarly weirdly condescendingly titled "We Are the World" ("We're saving our own lives," went the most notable line, as if Ethiopians were dying to give American pop stars entry into the kingdom of righteousness). Dylan was there, his singing a helpless self-parody so broad it would have gotten a comedian doing a Dylan impression, even

Richard Belzer, so brazen with his Yiddisha "Like a Rolling Stone," hooted off the stage.

He was in the deepest trough of the nadir of his career. For Bob Dylan the entire decade would be a continuing series of bad hair-dos and bad albums, both the hair-dos and the albums flailing for relevance—musical relevance, historical relevance, commercial relevance, just some reason to be noticed, it didn't matter—with flavor-of-the-month sidemen and producers, each new record greeted with cheering reviews, *This is it, this is the real comeback, not like the last one we said was the real comeback,* a true parade of sludge, the Christian albums *Slow Train Coming* in 1979, *Saved* in 1980, *Shot of Love* in 1981, then *Infidels* in 1983, *Empire Burlesque* in 1985, *Knocked Out Loaded* 1986, *Dylan and the Dead* 1988, *Down in the Groove* 1988, *Oh Mercy* 1989, *Under the Red Sky* 1990—featuring "T.V. Talkin' Song," "Handy Dandy," and "Wiggle Wiggle."

In 1965, in *The Success and Failure of Picasso,* John Berger told a strange story. After the Second World War, if not before, Picasso had become like King Midas: he could make so much money, by painting almost anything, that he could buy it. But since 1937, with the exploding mural *Guernica* and the comic strip *The Dream and Lie of Franco,* his life was a flailing for a subject: there was nothing he was actually impelled to paint. In the 1980s Bob Dylan was running on a parallel track, searching for a story to tell, something, anything, that would ring a gong, that would send out sound waves that might keep a song circling the earth forever, that might make a song part of history, or, perhaps greater, part of a life. Something that might live up to the credo the folk singer and song hunter Bascom Lamar Lunsford of North Carolina set out in the 1930s in his recital "In the Spirit of the Poet," his version of Long-fellow's "The Arrow and the Song":

> I shot an arrow into the air, it fell to earth I know not
> where;
> But years after still unbroken, I found that arrow in the
> heart of an oak.
>
> I breathed a song into the air, it fell to earth I know not
> where;
> But long years after from beginning to end,
> I found that song in the heart of a friend.

But at least on his records—for *Infidels* he made and then buried the song "Blind Willie McTell," which since a rehearsal with the guitarist Mark Knopfler appeared in 1991 has grown in people's hearts until it stands with if not above anything else he has ever done—Dylan had nothing worth a home in anyone's heart to sing about. Instead he was writing and recording hopeless songs, harmless soft protest about Catfish Hunter and Joey Gallo, Legionnaires' disease and the Rosenbergs, retreating into simple career-ism, taking the money, trying to wash it off his hands.

"I really was never any more than what I was—a folk musician who gazed into the gray mist with tear-blinded eyes and made up songs that floated in a luminous haze,"

Dylan wrote in *Chronicles,* but in the 1980s the haze was gone. "My fame was immense," he wrote of the time, "could fill a football stadium, but it was like having some weird diploma that won't get you into any college," and fame killed art: "Creativity has much to do with experience, observation and imagination, and if any one of those key elements is missing, it doesn't work. It was impossible now for me to observe anything without being observed." He pressed on harder: "I felt done for, an empty burned-out wreck. Too much static in my head and I couldn't dump the stuff. Wherever I am, I'm a '60s troubadour, a folk-rock relic, a wordsmith from bygone days, a fictitious head of state from a place nobody knows"—and with that swirlingly mysterious last clause hanging in the air, harder still: "The mirror had swung around and I could see the future—an old actor fumbling in garbage cans outside the theater of past triumphs." And down to earth, the language still alive, because he was looking back from 2004, to a time when he likely couldn't have written with such flair: "My live performances never seemed to capture the inner spirit of the songs . . . The windows had been boarded up for years and covered with cobwebs, and it's not like I didn't know it." And that is what he must have felt when, for one of the giant Live Aid relief concerts Bob Geldof organized for July 13, 1985—seventy-two thousand people at Wembley Stadium in London, more than eighty-nine thousand at John F. Kennedy Stadium in Philadelphia—he stepped onto the JFK stage with Keith Richards and Ron Wood of the Rolling Stones, the three of them carrying acoustic guitars. The performance was a debacle, high-lighted by Wood playing air guitar after handing his guitar to Dylan when Dylan broke a string on his own. It was only made worse by Jack Nicholson's beaming introduc-tion, his face bright with sincerity. "Some artists' work speaks for itself. Some artists speak for a generation," he said as applause began to rise like a building. "It is my deep personal pleasure to present to you one of America's great voices of freedom—IT CAN ONLY BE ONE MAN—THE TRANSCENDENT—BOB DYLAN!"

"Bob Dylan's eyes darted restlessly," the critic Jim Miller wrote. "Unshaven and puffy, his face poured sweat . . . He stumbled through a heartless version of his most famous song, 'Blowin' in the Wind.' The audience, responding to the nostalgia of the moment and the predictability of the gesture, cheered, as if on cue, as the scene was beamed by satellite around the world. At 46, Dylan was rock's unoffi-cial poet laureate. He looked like a waxen effigy." And he was, Miller argued: the performance had exposed him as someone who "matters less as a musician" than as a cross between a semiologist and an advertising agent, where music is merely a vehicle for a career of "giving form to passing fashions, epitomizing a certain style, defining a cutting edge for their audience." Now, "out of touch with his times, he had become irrelevant—a once brilliant manipulator of cultural signs, fated to produce cultural static"—the static that, as Dylan would write, at that time filled his own head.

And yet that was not the whole story of "Blowin' in

the Wind" at Live Aid, or perhaps even the real story at all. In a tape of the rehearsal Dylan, Richards, and Wood conducted, a tape that didn't surface until thirty-five years after the event, in 2020, you can hear something altogether different. You can hear a few people trying to find their way into an absolutely familiar song that resists them just as absolutely—*It's been more than twenty years I've been out there, you think you know all there is I know, you think you know what the answers are, don't you?*—and you can hear the three of them take pleasure in that rebuke, and rise to the challenge, and realize that it's not a challenge at all, that whatever they say will be right.

They fool with the song, finding their way into the melody, looking for openings, for its uncompleted structures. Their uncertainty creates delicacy and restraint. There's no way to tell whose guitar is leading, but there's an emphasis of regret in the way they let the melody lines close. You can follow them as they look for ways to let the melody snap back on itself—to make it new, or simply find a song they haven't heard before. Wood plays small flourishes that seem to lift the piece into an elegiac timelessness and that at the same time affirm that the song is a historical fact that everyone acknowledges without a second thought. And the longer they play, still with no one singing, the more "No More Auction Block" comes back.

"It's a beautiful song—I know people are a little bit wary about doing it," Wood says. "I think that on this occasion—" "Especially with just acoustic, too," Richards completes the thought, "this could be really nice." After almost five minutes they begin to find the song as Dylan brings the verses in, but as he steps through the words it feels as if he's reading off of a notepad where he's just scribbled them as they occurred to him. He is far back in the sound, standing in a doorway, halfway in the room and halfway out of it, encountering the song for the first time, stumbling on the questions with no clue about answers. The singing is in that luminous haze, so distant it seems without a body, and yet so confident, so *interested,* that the words can seem almost random: the drift in the melody as the three of them have found it, as they try to follow its meanderings, is everything. And you can imagine that if they'd come out and performed the song as they were playing it in that moment, the reaction would have been the same as it was at the Newport Folk Festival in 1965, when in the temple of the true folk Dylan appeared with a rock 'n' roll band so loud he had to sing right through it and against the noise people in the crowd booed and cursed, but now that event reversed so completely it might as well be silent: *We can't hear him! Can't hear the words! Down with abstraction!* Even if they're playing on acoustic guitars to show some folkie respect.

"Gotta take the tape," Dylan says as they finish.[*]

---

[*] The tape is full of surprises. At about sixteen minutes in they work up "Ballad of Hollis Brown," and Richards identifies the switchback rhythm: not "Pretty Polly," the song's obvious foundation, but Elvis's "You're Right, I'm Left, She's Gone." Eleven minutes later they go back to "Blowin' in the Wind," with Richards singing in a reedy voice: "E minus," he says, "Peter Paul & Mary did it—just a straight C," as if for him that's the real pop reference point for the song, not Dylan's *Freewheelin'* recording. A few minutes

There's the signal performance on November 4, 2008, election day, at Northrop Auditorium, on the campus of the University of Minnesota, where Bob Dylan registered in the fall of 1959, when Eisenhower was still president—going on fifty years, his first performance at his erstwhile alma mater. "Blowin' in the Wind" was the last song. Dylan introduced his band in a boosted voice. "I was born in 1941, the year they bombed Pearl Harbor," he said in a toast-master mode, as if he were bringing on Marilyn Monroe's Society Syncopators from *Some Like It Hot,* the same lines every night. "I've been living in a world of darkness ever since," he said, still not dropping the pose. "But it looks like things are going to change now," he said, as if that would make a difference, as if he'd notice if things did.[†]

————

later Wood takes the vocal for "Hollis Brown," then Dylan. "I don't sing it the same way all the time," he says, hearing something new in the song. "It's like 'Little Maggie,' " he says, and he rolls right into it, with Richards playing as if he's done the old Appalachian lament of a man in love with a woman who's thrown away her life for half of his: " 'Oh yonder stands Little Maggie, with a shot glass in her hand / She's drinkin' away her troubles, with a low down gamblin' man.' "

[†] For all the costumed slickness, it wasn't as if there wasn't a whole view of the world behind what Dylan said that night. "Rock and roll was indeed an extension of what was going on—the big swinging bands—Ray Noble, Will Bradley, Glenn Miller, I listened to that music before I heard Elvis Presley," he said in 2017. "But rock and roll was high energy, explosive and cut down. It was skeleton music, came out of the darkness and rode in on the atom bomb and the artists were star headed like mystical Gods. Rhythm and blues, country and western, bluegrass and gospel were always there—but it was compartmentalized—it was great but it wasn't dangerous. Rock and roll was a dangerous weapon, chrome plated, it exploded like the speed

Then he dropped the act and sang the song in an accusatory voice, as if it were "Masters of War" and he knew who was to blame, as if it really was supposed to answer him, as if the song itself knew why the world was out of joint. The pace was broken, then picking up, smoothing itself out, almost stopping: he was almost pantomiming the song. In the shifting tones of his voice, he could have been a backwoods philosopher reciting "When Last We Met at the Garden Gate" or Bert Parks crooning "There She Is, Miss America."‡ The last verse finished, he followed the harmonica out the door and into the future. When Barack Obama gave his victory speech that night in Grant Park, he quoted Sam Cooke's "A Change Is Gonna Come." Cooke always said it was "Blowin' in the Wind" that inspired

----

of light, it reflected the times, especially the presence of the atomic bomb which had preceded it by several years. Back then people feared the end of time. The big showdown between capitalism and communism was on the horizon. Rock and roll made you oblivious to the fear, busted down the barriers that race and religion, ideologies put up. We lived under a death cloud; the air was radioactive. There was no tomorrow, any day it could all be over, life was cheap. That was the feeling at the time and I'm not exaggerating. Doo-wop was the counterpart to rock and roll. Songs like 'In the Still of the Night,' 'Earth Angel,' 'Thousand Miles Away,' those songs balanced things out, they were heartfelt and melancholy for a world that didn't seem to have a heart. The doo-wop groups might have been an extension, too, of the Ink Spots and gospel music, but it didn't matter; that was brand new too. Groups like the Five Satins and the Meadowlarks seemed to be singing from some imaginary street corner down the block."

‡ Or for that matter "Maggie's Farm," which in 1981, in *The Freshman*, Parks boomed off a stage at a dinner where only endangered species were served.

him to write it, that challenged him to go farther. He felt shamed that it took a white person to write a song that said what this song said; he saw how big a hit it was, how many people wanted to hear a song like that. But if Dylan truly had left the song unfinished, so that history could finish it, as on this night the song addressed an election and an election addressed the song, the tale "Blowin' in the Wind" tells might have achieved a deeper focus in *One Night in Miami,* a movie released in January 2021, between the defeat of Donald Trump and the inauguration of Joe Biden, when the old story about Sam Cooke and "Blowin' in the Wind" was played out as a true vortex of history. That it was all made up, Regina King directing and screen-writer Kemp Powers adapting his own play, didn't matter; "Blowin' in the Wind" was made up. "Blowin' in the Wind" gave its account of history, and made an argument about what history was; the picture did the same.

It's the night of February 25, 1964, and Cassius Clay, twenty-two, played by Eli Goree; Sam Cooke, thirty-three, played Leslie Odom Jr.; Jim Brown, twenty-eight, played by Aldis Hodge; and Malcolm X, thirty-eight, played by Kingsley Ben-Adir, are together in Malcolm's rooms in the Hampton House Motel in the Overtown neighborhood of Miami, the black part of town. Taking the heavyweight championship from Sonny Liston, Clay has just defied the expectations of the world. The rest were all there to see it happen. Now they're together to celebrate, but the mood is off. Malcolm digs into Cooke for selling out to white people: "*Mr. Soul,*" he says mordantly. He's got a portable phonograph; he pulls out a Cooke album, places it on the turntable, and puts the needle down on the 1957 number one "You Send Me," and lets the smooth, creamy voice play for a moment. "Or maybe this one," he says smilingly, but with a hint of the kill behind it, picking up the needle and dropping it on another hit from the same year, "(I Love You) For Sentimental Reasons"—which begins with Cooke mindlessly burbling "I love you" more than a dozen times, and coming off the screen it feels both shameless and ridiculous. Malcolm laughs softly, as at a private joke. "Your music is *deep,* brother," he says. They argue. Cooke has a message, he says: he's his own man. *I can stand up in front of white people and beat them at their own game.* Malcolm reaches into a closet and fishes out another LP. "You know," he says serenely, "I was thinking about this song I heard on the radio the other day." He's holding a disc with a red Columbia label. "It's a song that made me think of you. Turns out it's pretty popular." You hear the needle touch the groove.

It can freeze you cold, as the first strums of "Blowin' in the Wind" come into the room, creating a whole new world in those few notes, a world that transforms the room, as the room, with these men gathered in it in fiction, transforms the song. It's Kemp Powers introducing the iconic song, in 2021, with nearly sixty years of made history behind it, back into the 1964 of the story, the song existing in the breach in history the song has already made, Powers inserting the song into his version of an iconic night, which makes a scramble of the iconic. Here it is all immediate, happening as you watch, nothing abstract, no theory of sign and act: you can physically feel the song entering into history, but you can also feel history entering into the song. It's Clay, Brown, Malcolm, and Cooke gathered around the little record player that make the song seem so big, so different, as it translates the language they've been speaking, and their presence translates the song into a different language, a bigger language, than any it has spoken before.

And then Kingsley Ben-Adir's Malcolm X, or Regina King, or Kemp Powers, hears a different song than anyone has heard before. Bending his neck down, Malcolm begins to nod to the music. Dylan sings "How many roads" and Malcolm points his finger in Cooke's face. Malcolm begins to softly bop around the room, hitting Cooke again with an exaggerated stare. Then a smile covers his face as he begins to snap his fingers, still bopping, awkwardly, he's no dancer, but as he does so he expands the music. He's heard the big beat.

Again he wags a finger in Cooke's face. "Uh! Unh, unh!" Cooke looks angry, silenced, angry at being silenced, not by Malcolm, but by the song: all resentment and ambition, Odom brings something of his Aaron Burr in *Hamilton* to the moment. "Oooo! I *love* those lyrics!" Malcolm crows. "Especially at the beginning. 'How many roads can a man walk down before you can call him a man'—how much do the oppressed have to take before they can be *recognized* as human *beings?*" "I heard it when it first came out," Cooke says, in a voice that barely makes it out of his throat. "Did it anger you?" Again in a half voice: "Why should it?" "This Bob Dylan fellow, a white boy from Minnesota?" "So what?" Malcolm picks up the album sleeve: "This is a white boy, from *Minnesota,* who has *nothing* to gain, from writing a song that speaks more to the struggles of our people than anything that you have ever penned in *your life.* I know I can't be the shrewd business person that you are, my brother, but since you *say* being involved in the struggle is bad for business, why is this son of a gun higher in the pop charts than anything you got out?"

Sam Cooke was shot to death in a motel in South Central Los Angeles at the end of the year, on December 11, 1964. Bob Dylan is still singing "Blowin' in the Wind," and as other people continue to record their own versions, they may be hoping it will reflect history back on them, making them feel part of it, maybe figuring that it will affirm that as the history in the song remains to be made, people might still respond, and they'll make it a hit all over again. Bob Dylan may have had nothing to gain when he wrote "Blowin' in the Wind"—what has he gained since? Ten million dollars? Twenty million? And if in 2020, fifty-five years after he was assassinated as he spoke at a gathering of his Organization of Afro-American Unity in the Audubon Ballroom in New York City on February 21, 1965, Malcolm X had been present to read that Bob Dylan had sold his entire catalogue of songs to the Universal Music Group, the biggest music company on the planet, for hundreds of millions of dollars, do you think he would be staring at the wall in his apartment back in Omaha, cursing how naïve he'd been? Or do you think that, knowing full well where that melody came from, he wouldn't begrudge the singer a dime?

* * *

"The supreme moment of this national séance, in which the summons of folksong to the cultural dead populated the stage with a reunited family of heroes and heroines of the past," Robert Cantwell wrote in 1996, speaking of the whole sweep of what was called the folk revival of the late 1950s and early sixties, "occurred at the closing concert of the Newport Folk Festival in 1963. Pete Seeger, Bob Dylan, Joan Baez, and Peter, Paul, and Mary linked arms with SNCC's Freedom Singers to sing the old Baptist hymn, 'We Shall Overcome,' and a parable of apocalypse, Bob Dylan's 'Blowin' in the Wind'—litanies of the revival's dream of freedom, brotherhood, and peace. It was a moment," Cantwell put down, "in which, like a celestial syzygy, many independent forces of tradition, ideology, and culture, wandering at large in time, some of them in historical deep space and others only transient displays in the contemporary cultural atmosphere, briefly converged to reveal the truth of our collective life."*

---

* "Peter, Paul, and Mary, for example, who looked like seminarians and bore New Testament names," Cantwell continued, "might have flourished on the Christian Missionary Youth circuit. At a deeper level, the dust-bowl balladeer, Woody Guthrie, was present in spirit, as was the wandering Swedenborgian, Johnny Appleseed. But so were the Fisk Jubilee Singers of

Mavis Staples, with whom a teenage Bob Dylan had fallen in love after hearing her singing on the Staple Singers' "Uncloudy Day" in 1960, could speak for many of those present that night, and many of those Cantwell heard behind them. "How could he write, 'How many roads must a man walk down, before you can call him a man?'" she said in 2005, more than four decades after the Staple Singers had recorded the song. "That is what my *father* went through. He was the one who wasn't called a man. So, how, where is he coming from? *White people don't have hard times*—that was my thinkin', back then, because I was a kid, too. What he was writing was *inspirational* . . . It's the same as gospel. He was writing *truth*." Thirteen years later, at the Xcel Center in St. Paul, Mavis Staples and Bob Dylan were touring together. In 1963, he had wanted to marry her. She said she was too young—and she couldn't see herself marrying somebody white. Now

---

the 1870s and the Almanac Singers of the 1940s, after whom the Freedom Singers, at Seeger's suggestion, had modeled themselves; Tom Joad and James Dean were present in spirit, as was a dark Pocahontas with a Spanish name in the guise of a demure schoolgirl singing an Elizabethan ballad and dreaming of its hero, a dashing gypsy laddie. Perhaps Holden Caulfield, from Pencey Prep, was in attendance too: not out of Salinger's novel but in the unwritten sequel that Dylan, who once dreamed of playing Holden in a movie, was enacting in his own life. Others, less palpable perhaps, lingered around the group—a Puritan man of the cloth, a plantation slave, a Jehovah's Witness, a blackface minstrel with a banjo—all of them held together with the vast chorus of the audience whose 15,000 voices ascended into the summer night." As for Peter, Paul & Mary as seminarians, I can't resist the late Ralph J. Gleason's glimpse of the same thing: "Two rabbis and a hooker don't make it."

she sang "Freedom Highway": "March for freedom highway / March each and every day / The whole world is wondering / What's wrong with the U.S.A." Once that last line referenced Emmett Till; in 2018, with the Voting Rights Act of 1965 eviscerated, with black people throughout the South gerrymandered off the electoral map, with proud white Nazis marching with arms through Thomas Jefferson's hometown, it didn't need to. With her band vamping behind her, in a kind of call and response with herself, she gave a speech about how Pops Staples had written "Freedom Highway" in 1965 for the March from Selma to Montgomery: "I was *there,* and I'm still here. I'm a living witness. I'm a soldier." She summoned the presence to fill the hall with history that was made, and history that was being unmade. It was very overdone, very show biz, and it was true. Even if you couldn't get out from under what an act it was, it was impossible not to be humbled. "Is this your first Bob Dylan show?" someone asked an older couple. "Yes," they said. "But we never miss Mavis."

History in the unmaking was the movie running behind the news two years later. You could see it anywhere. You could hear it anywhere. "I grew up a long time ago, in the sixties," Mike Krzyzewski said on August 27, 2020, at a Black Lives Matter protest in Durham, North Carolina, organized by Henry Coleman III of Coach K's Duke University basketball team, two days after Jacob Blake of Kenosha, Wisconsin, was shot seven times in the back by a white police officer. "I thought it was heading in the right direction. Damn, I was wrong."

* * *

The song had traveled the same road, holding its shape even when it was no longer a song, when it was just ordinary language. A few months before Krzyzewski spoke, on June 2, a week after George Floyd died under the knee of a police officer at the intersection of Chicago Avenue and East 38th Street in Minneapolis, the NPR reporter Noel King spoke to Minnesota State Representative Ruth Richardson about why it was no longer safe for her son, Shawn, a high-school sprinter, to run alone in their neighborhood in Mendota Heights, a small town, as it advertised itself, "between Minneapolis and St. Paul": "You can't," Richardson told her son, "do the same things that your white friends do." "If I can't run in the neighborhood," Shawn Richardson told King, "it's like I can run on a track or something. You know, it's not the end of the world." "It is the end of the world," Ruth Richardson answered. "Because if you can't run in our neighborhood, if you can't walk out into the world, and just be seen as a seventeen-year-old boy who loves to run, there's something deeply wrong with that."

"What do you think the right response is?" King asked later. "To address racism in our country?" Richardson said. "I mean, that's a really big question, because, look: you can change legislation, but you can't change hearts and minds. When I visited the site of George Floyd's death, there was a sign that said SMASH WHITE SUPREMACY. And as I was watching the sign just kind of blowing in the wind—it was on a white sheet and spray-painted with red letters—it was like the answer is literally blowing in the wind at the site of where George Floyd was murdered."

It was, in a way, as if "No More Auction Block" had returned to claim the song that had begun in the skin of its melody, or anyway to return the new song to its own origins, to that time when history seemed to be moving in the right direction. "The systems that we have built within this country have been built with racism at the core," Richardson said finally, in her political voice, with a cadence that allowed her to sing the song in her own way. "People talk about our systems being broken. Our systems are working just the way that they were designed to work."

THE LONESOME
DEATH OF
HATTIE CARROLL

1964

When I started writing about music, in 1965, music and politics—music as a form of the argument over the good, over how to make a commonwealth where all might find a way to see the good plain, but also the music in politics, the presence of harmony and dissonance as people argued over this election, that law, that speech, the crowd's response—was all I wrote about. It seemed then that the connections between the two were simple, obvious, and overwhelming. There was a sense of change beginning to gather force—and everything was part of it. There were no barriers between what, now, might be called different forms of discourse. You couldn't talk about anything—the Top 40, Lyndon Johnson, movies, nineteenth-century novels, the Vietnam War, architecture, marriage, school, food, or even the weather—without talking about everything else. ("We made love last night," a friend said of his wife and himself at the time. "I couldn't help it, I shouted out, 'Take that, LBJ!'") Everything was held together, made into a single subject. That came from that sense of the world out of joint, of fear and jeopardy and absolute uncertainty, the immediate legacy of the assassination of President Kennedy in 1963. With the civil rights movement blocked from outside and fragmenting within, it came from a sense of a country where promises were made and promises were broken, or betrayed. It came from an unending war that, for those born just before or during World War II, or in the glow that victory over evil left behind, was discrediting the country with its own evil, bringing the whole idea of the country into question. Nothing was finished, and everything was linked to everything else because all these things were an engine of history, powering a sense that history was unwritten, that it was being written as you or anyone else walked down the street, with the street now transformed into a combination of theater and public square.

A deep feeling for history, the legacy that the past gives to the present, the legacy and burden of keeping the promises the past made, or refuting them for good, coupled with an awareness of the peculiar contingency of any present moment, has always been at the heart of the best criticism. A year later, I discovered Pauline Kael's *I Lost It at the Movies;* she'd been writing that way since the mid-fifties, mostly in pieces squirreled off in hard-to-find film journals or broadcasts on a left-wing Berkeley FM radio station when few people knew what the FM on their radio was for, the same station that was playing Bob Dylan's "Blowin' in the Wind" in 1963. "It is a no and *somebody* has to say it," she said in 1955 in "The Glamour of Delinquency." "For the first time in American history we have a widespread nihilistic movement, so nihilistic it doesn't even have a program, and, ironically, its only leader is a movie star: Marlon Brando." Now that enveloping critical voice was everywhere. It was everyday talk.

That voice was something you could catch every time you turned on AM radio, whether you were hearing the Beatles, the Rolling Stones, the Miracles, the Animals, the Supremes, or a hundred other people, half of whom, it seemed, you hadn't heard of the day before. The voice was something that Scoop Nisker, who had gone to summer camp with Bob Dylan and seemed to take that as something to live up to, caught in the line that closed his breakneck free-form collage newscasts on KMPX and KSAN in San Francisco: "If you don't like the news, go out and make some of your own." That could mean making a record, organizing a demonstration, opening a restaurant, or writing a piece about any of those things that ended up being about all of them.

This is what it sounded like, what it felt like. Here again is Sandy Darlington, who died in 1989 at fifty-four, writing in 1968 in the *San Francisco Express-Times* about what some people were calling the counterculture and what he called "the Community," a commonwealth where people were looking for the good, writing about that and about

Cream—the guitarist Eric Clapton, the bassist Jack Bruce, who died in 2014 at seventy-one, and the drummer Ginger Baker, who died in 2019 at eighty, three musicians from England who by the name they chose for themselves were saying, *You want to hear the best music in the world? We'll play it for you*—and about the band's first appearance in San Francisco, at Winterland Ballroom, an ice-skating palace now transformed into what to Darlington was a refugee camp for people "dropping out of a world that says Remember the Maine into one that says Remember Huck Finn," "a kind of immigrant processing and indoctrination center like the Lower East Side used to be. Long lines flow out of the doors into the street, like a photo of breadlines in the thirties."

Darlington described what it meant for the people in Cream, born during or just before the Second World War, to grow up in postwar Britain: rationing that lasted into the 1950s, bombs exploding in the ruins that still covered working-class London neighborhoods, a class-based education system: "If you flunk the exams they give you at age eleven, you are channeled toward a trade. You apprentice at fourteen or fifteen for several years, at the end of which time you are a certified metal lathe-worker and will be until you die." The people in Cream were in their twenties in 1968, but to Darlington they carried a longer history in their faces, just as their music wiped history off the books and left the future a white page on which you could write whatever you chose. Darlington heard *Plessy v. Ferguson;* he heard the Treaty of Versailles. Today you can so easily go online and hear the show Darlington was writing about, all shocking fury, an attack that drove a song like a tank, flew it like a dive bomber, a music that if it could be summed up in a phrase might be *No end in sight.*

Their clothes will always seem a bit baggy. They look and act like medieval British peasants must have done who gathered together on the festival of the Great Wren on St. Stephen's Day and tore apart a wren which they believed had magical powers, and divided the bits and pieces among themselves, the poor. Or like those British people who still practice fertility rites such as singing to the apple trees on May Day and pouring cider over them to convince them to bear fruit once more.

Their faces are bony and shaggy and they absorb the light and create huge hollows of shadow around themselves as though they are always walking down narrow foggy dank streets lit by gaslight, like characters out of Dickens.

All this directness and savagery and determination comes out in the music, and it speaks to us of the Community who gather at Winterland to hear them. Things like Versailles and Segregation affected Cream and Otis Redding, and now they in turn are affecting us. Week after week we go inside the music, and as they play and we listen and dance, the questions and ideas slowly germinate in our minds like seeds: This is our school, our summit conference. This music is more than entertainment. It describes and helps us to define a way of life we believe in. So what are we going to do about it? The Cream along with Lyndon and the Mayor are helping us to plan our summer.

"A way of life we believe in"—to Aristotle, to the thinkers of the Enlightenment, politics meant the creation of civil society. It meant the public life everyone shares with everyone else, whether that means a Pericles speaking in the Agora, Samuel Danforth's Election Day sermon in Boston in 1670, children lining up to drink their polio vaccine in paper cups in 1955, a Sunday promenade in Bologna, a high-school football game in Texas, a party convention, trying a new restaurant, attending a concert by Eagles of Death Metal, or sitting at home watching the news of a terrorist attack in the Batacalan in Paris where Eagles of Death Metal were playing and eighty-nine people died— that was civil society, and civil society meant the field where the good could be discovered and lived out. What was the good? It was what Adams, Jefferson, Madison, and Hamilton called civic virtue, the apprehension of right and wrong and living out the right—as in the old American phrase "living on the square," which can mean both living life with honesty and living life in public, in full view of others, not hiding, not masked, on the public square. It was each person's pursuit of one's own true self and acknowledging the true self of whoever one might meet.

It meant not talking falsely, and trying to discover what it was one truly wanted to say and how to say it. As a friend once said of the political theorist Hannah Arendt's right society—the society that would flower when what she called the social question, the question of want, of food, shelter, literacy, and dignity, had been settled—politics would mean the people of a community coming together to decide what plays to put on, which is not far from the scene Sandy Darlington set more than half a century ago.

Half a century later the social question hangs over everything else—in its modern form as the monetization of all activity and speech and the division of society into winners and losers. "In this corrupt society / The rich / Pay to be free," the punk band Rubella Ballet sang in "Money Talks" in 1988, but three decades later, as Ivanka Trump and Jared Kushner glided through the White House as if it might well have been the Palace of Versailles, the rich were paid to be free, to represent freedom to everyone else. The social question governs our politics and poisons our talk. It perverts our sense of justice and our ability to even acknowledge one another, to the point that politics has broken down into a war over who deserves the good, and who doesn't: "most people living in the United States today," wrote one Glenn Ellmers, in a journal that called itself *The American Mind,* in 2021, "—certainly more than half—are not Americans in any meaningful sense of the term." But the question of what plays to put on is as central in the twenty-first century as it was in Athens in the fifth century B.C.—and one way of deciding what plays to put on is deciding what songs to make, or to listen to.

In such a frame of mind each song becomes a play,

and each song is then a failed or a successful attempt to dramatize life, to speak without falsehood to an audience the person making the song wants to reach. If you think about it that way, if you listen that way, listen to your favorite song that way, then no song is simple. No song is just a song. No song exists outside of politics—outside of what is better called the political, a certain dimension of life in which people of a certain commonality come together to decide what to do with their shared space and time. Any song captures the good or its opposite—or creates an image of the good that we can reach for, be humbled by, be humiliated by our failure to achieve it. Such as Bob Dylan's "The Lonesome Death of Hattie Carroll," written in the late summer of 1963 and released in 1964 on his earnest and humorless social-question third album, *The Times They Are A-Changin'*, and, just short of twenty years later, Laurie Anderson's 1981 "O Superman." In some ways they could not be more different. Dylan's song came out of the topical social-protest stream of the Greenwich Village folk milieu, and adopts the voice of Woody Guthrie's "Ludlow Massacre." Anderson's song came out of the New York milieu of galleries and artists' nightclubs, and uses the diffident, ironic voice of the avant-garde from Gérard de Nerval on down. But they are also the same song. "O Superman" may never have taken shape without "The Lonesome Death of Hattie Carroll" echoing in cultural memory, and "O Superman" can dramatize how hard "The Lonesome Death of Hattie Carroll" really is.

I first saw Bob Dylan at a Joan Baez concert in a field in

New Jersey in the summer of 1963. When I got back to California I went to a record store in the Stanford Shopping Center in Palo Alto and asked for a Bob Dylan album—though I probably asked for a Bob Die-lan album—and came home with *The Freewheelin' Bob Dylan*. It was funny and searing, full of wordplay and fearsome. The songs on the vinyl didn't match the songs listed on the album cover, but I didn't care. After that *The Times They Are A-Changin'* seemed one-dimensional, but "The Lonesome Death of Hattie Carroll" pushed so fiercely into the one dimension of the album, the dimension of justice, that categories broke down and anything you might bring to the song came flooding back as you listened. You were implicated in the drama. You were forced into every role, and there was no exit.

I've been listening to this song, writing about it, playing it back in memory—because of the way the song is made, as the deliberate cadence of each word calls up the next, the song locks in—for coming on to sixty years. But in 2019, at one point on a driving trip in Minnesota, with a driver's soundtrack that included a lot of Lana Del Rey and a lot of Bob Dylan—of course his song "Highway 61 Revisited," from 1965, as there we were, on the North Shore, Lake Superior on the right, up from Duluth toward the Canadian border on that very two-lane strip of asphalt—"Hattie Carroll" came on, and it was as if I'd never heard it before.

At the time Bob Dylan wrote it, the connection between music and politics, in some realms of public life, was absolute. Along with other members of CORE, Suze Rotolo was

sitting in at Woolworth's in New York to protest its segre-
gated lunch counters in the South; she opened Bob Dylan's
eyes and opened his door to history, the history that was
being made between them and around them. Dylan was
writing songs about the Bomb—some of them thirdhand
and puerile, and one, a mad Lenny Bruce–like routine
where he fell in love with it, and spoke in its voice, hilar-
ious—and about the civil rights movement. They were
solemn songs that began in 1962 with the unreleased
'twas-down-in-Mississippi-not-so-long-ago "The Death
of Emmett Till," a slow, measured drone where the body
of the fourteen-year-old boy from Chicago, murdered by
white men in Money, Mississippi, on August 28, 1955, after
he spoke to a white woman, was placed on the body of
Dave Van Ronk's version of the prostitute's ballad "House
of the Rising Sun." On July 6, 1963, with Pete Seeger, the
folk singer Judy Collins, and the folk singer and actor Theodore Bikel, Dylan was in Greenwood, Mississippi, near
where Robert Johnson was killed in 1938—as Dylan had
spoken of writing "The Death of Robert Johnson," that
notion, it seems, turned into "The Death of Emmett Till."
Dylan and the others were there for a voter registration
rally organized by SNCC—at that time and place, an event
that could all but promise that violence if not death would
be visited on those behind it, once the famous white people present had gone back to New York. Later that day
Dylan sat down and played with a small gathering of com-
rades, including Bernice Johnson Reagon of the Albany
Singing Movement and the SNCC Freedom Singers, with

whom he would link arms and share a stage at the New-port Folk Festival not three weeks later to sing "Blowin' in the Wind" and "We Shall Overcome."*

This day, for a crowd of some three hundred sharecrop-pers, ringed by a few robed Klansmen, Dylan was singing the song that appeared on *The Times They Are A-Changin'* as "Only a Pawn in Their Game," but on the sixth of July was called "The Death of Medgar Evers," after the Missis-sippi civil rights leader who had been shot in the back as he approached his front door in Jackson, Mississippi, on the twelfth of June, barely more than three weeks before. It wasn't a "finger-pointing song," as Dylan would later dismiss his protest music. It was a structural analysis of the social mechanics of southern racism that somehow still felt personal, the act of a particular person who, con-fronted with a soul-chilling assassination, had actually sat

* "I ran into Al Grossman," Bikel, a veteran of civil rights activity in the South, recalled nearly five decades after the fact. "I said to him, look. Dylan's been writing these songs of social awareness, and they're important songs and people start to sing them, as part of their arsenal, their weap-onry, in the service of the Civil Rights movement. But he really doesn't have firsthand experience about where it's happening . . . And I think he should go. And Grossman says, he's just starting to work in small clubs. He can't afford to fly down to Mississippi. I wrote out a check, I gave it to Grossman, I said, buy him a ticket. This is the flight I'm going on. Book him on this flight. We'll go down together. Don't tell him where the money came from. Just buy him the ticket. Sure. So Dylan and I sat on the flight, it was an evening flight, for the night before the mass meeting. And he was writing these lyrics on the back of old envelopes. And I remember saying to him, I'd like to see the lyrics you're going to write on the way *back*. I think that was the last time Dylan was actively, proactively, engaged in the movement." Bikel died in 2015 at ninety-one.

down to think about it, and who had come up with a point of view that wasn't obvious. The focus of the song wasn't really on Medgar Evers at all. It was on the working-class white man who, in a drama playing out in Dylan's mind, was both killer and victim. In terms of legal facts, Dylan was wrong: Byron De La Beckwith, who killed Medgar Evers, was a rich man and a Klan leader who everyone knew was guilty, who walked off laughing after hanging two juries, who would not go to prison until 1994, dying in custody in 2001 at eighty, when Medgar Evers would have been seventy-five. It wasn't much of a song. It had a hectoring melody, and nothing that could be called a rhythm. Its structural analysis was sentimental: even if the man who shot Medgar Evers was an illiterate white share-cropper trying to prove he was better than a black lawyer, as Salman Rushdie once put it—during that time when Rushdie could not show his face, when he could not stand in the public square—"The responsibility for violence lies with those who perpetrate it." All those weaknesses may be why the song can seem to have little presence today. But in 1963 the song rang true. It rang true because you could sense someone looking, putting himself in the place of someone else, seeing what that imaginary person would have seen, and seeing what they didn't.

From the poverty shacks, he looks from the cracks to the
   tracks
And the hoofbeats pound in his brain
And he's taught how to walk in a pack

Shoot in the back
With his fist in a clinch
To hang and to lynch
To hide 'neath the hood
To kill with no pain
Like a dog on a chain
He ain't got no name
But it ain't him to blame
He's only a pawn in their game

Putting himself in someone else's place—that allowed anyone listening to put him- or herself in any place occupied by anyone in the song. "The first time I heard the song, I was maybe 16 or 17 years old," the jazz trumpeter Christian Scott aTunde Adjuah, born in 1983, wrote in 2021 on the occasion of Bob Dylan's eightieth birthday. "The first time I had a police officer pull a gun on me, I was walking home from school. I was about 13 years old. The song broke down that cognitive dissonance that can easily be created in this country, where you think only people who look like you have your perspective or can see your experience. I heard those things coming out of the mouth of a person where, if you put me in a lineup next to him, you might arguably say we had completely contrasting experiences. But here it was that this person was able to see what those people were enduring in that moment and took some agency in being clear that that wasn't the right way." And the sense of changing places was there when Adjuah first saw the cover of *The Times They Are A-Changin'*:

"Seeing another kid, another teenager, that had the ability to see these things in that moment—to be able to see *me*—is something that engendered him to me. I will always be grateful to him. He's one of the pillars of my musical life, because of his willingness to speak truth and be morally upright during his experience in this place."

The song was cruel, refusing its own righteousness, stating plainly that nothing would change: the last verse returned to Medgar Evers, for his funeral, with the same last line carried by every verse now on his tombstone: ONLY A PAWN IN THEIR GAME. This was the dynamic of the moment. As events tumbled out of real life from wherever they came from and passed through Bob Dylan in New York and then began to travel the land as songs, Bob Dylan was living his life as much as a medium as he was a song-writer.

He was in Washington, D.C., the nation's capital, on August 28 of the same year, a month after Newport, not two months after Greenwood, eight years to the day after Emmett Till was dumped in the Tallahatchie River, an anniversary lost on few of the hundreds of thousands present, to sing at the March on Washington for Jobs and Freedom—an event history would mark as the apogee of the civil rights movement. Introduced by the actor Ossie Davis as already someone who "needs no further intro-duction," he sang "Only a Pawn in Their Game." With Joan Baez keening in a piercing, almost mystical voice beside him, he sang "When the Ship Comes In," a promise of justice and vengeance rooted in Bertolt Brecht and Kurt

Weill's "Pirate Jenny," which he'd learned from Rotolo's album of *The Threepenny Opera*. With the powerful Len Chandler leading, with Baez, Bikel, the Freedom Singers, and Peter, Paul & Mary, he sang the freedom song "Eyes on the Prize." Peter, Paul & Mary had already sung their hit "Blowin' in the Wind."

As Dylan left the gathering on a bus, the story goes, he read a story in the local newspaper. On that same day—the day Martin Luther King Jr. gave the speech where he proclaimed a dream of an America that finally lived up to its promises—a panel of three judges in Maryland had concluded a case in which a man named William Zantzinger had been charged with the murder of a fifty-one-year-old hotel worker named Hattie Carroll. He was at a party in Baltimore, he was drunk, she didn't bring him a drink fast enough, he cursed her, he called her a n-----, he hit her on the neck with a toy cane, and within hours she was dead of a heart attack. Having reduced the charge to manslaughter, the judges remanded Zantzinger, an aristocratic tobacco farmer, to the county jail, delaying his time until after the fall, so that he could oversee the harvest of his crop. So Dylan decided to try to tell that story in a song, changing the name to Zanzinger, letting the word slide more easily into whatever word would come next. He decided to put on that play. "I wrote 'Hattie Carroll' in a small notebook in a restaurant on 7th Avenue," Dylan said in 1985. "I'd had the information beforehand and people were talking about it . . . I felt I had a lot in common with this situation and was able to manifest my feelings. The set pattern to the song I think is based on Brecht, 'The Ship, the Black Freighter' "—another name for "Pirate Jenny."

That day in Minnesota all I could hear was the perfection of the song as a work of art—of how, perhaps, the horror of the event brought out an apotheosis of craft that Dylan had never quite found before and would never find again. All I could hear was a few minutes of the sort of aesthetic measuring and balancing necessary to write two people who would have otherwise been forgotten into history, and write a song that would itself become part of history, and make its own history.*

There was the direct opening line of each verse, then the music opening up for a detailed narrative, then the chorus undermining what you had just heard and speeding you into the next verse—speaking a different language, almost becoming a different language. Every word stood out of the song as a visitation, as if it were being received by the songwriter, not made, and at the same time every shift in vocal intonation stood out as a choice. You could follow the slow climb of each verse, lining out a story of

---

* If Dylan meant to secure Hattie Carroll's place in history, it's hard to imagine he meant to do the same for William Zantzinger, but he did. Zantzinger walked out of jail to live an ugly life of privilege and fraud. He went back to jail—though only for overnight stays—for extorting rents from impoverished black families on property he did not even own. He never escaped the song. He died at sixty-nine in 2009. To the end he cursed Dylan for making sure his name would outlive him. "He's a no-account son of a bitch," he said nearly forty years after Dylan, in his way, imprisoned him. "He's like the scum of a bag of the earth."

injustice that as one followed another made the story of a single life, up a staircase. You could feel how the unfinished judgment of the chorus met each verse at the landing—

And you who philosophize disgrace
And criticize all fears

—and anyone could remember the outrage, the fright, felt at a headline that made one feel filthy, obscene, even to read it, and the shrug from someone else, a professor, a boss, a relative, saying, *You'll learn,* and your fear that you would—

Take the rag away from your face
Now ain't the time for your tears

You could hear the chorus then sending the song down to begin the climb again, and it felt like a kind of miracle: *how could anyone simply* think *of that?* "You've got to have power and dominion over the spirits," Dylan wrote in *Chronicles* of what it took to write "Masters of War," "A Hard Rain's A-Gonna Fall," and "The Lonesome Death of Hattie Carroll"—a power, he said, that in 1963 and 1964 had come and gone, that he knew he would never get back. But he was also saying that at that time the spirits—the spirits of his time and place, the United States in the mid-sixties—had power and dominion over him.

When Bob Dylan performed the song at Carnegie Hall

in 1963, the last verse and chorus are all force and brutality and scorn, as if to disguise the singer's disgust at his own tune. It's horrifying, and when the crowd applauds at the end of the song it feels all wrong, like a violation, as if the people in the audience think the song was congratulating them, as if when Dylan sings "You who philosophize disgrace" he's talking about someone else. On Highway 61 all those years later, when that self-congratulation had become its own form of discourse, when in universities and in journalism people were bullied out of the public square so that others could proclaim their own purity, there was no someone else. There was no way out of the song. We listened in complete silence, as if we were holding our breath, as if we didn't know how the tragedy would conclude, as if we didn't know all the lines of the play by heart, as if we'd never heard the last chorus not merely turn the last verse back down the stairs but grab it by the neck and throw it down until it lay crumpled up dead on the first step:

> In the courtroom of honor, the judge pounded his gavel
> To show that all's equal and that the courts are on the level
> And that the strings in the books ain't pulled and per-
> suaded
> And that even the nobles get properly handled
> Once that the cops have chased after and caught 'em
> And that the ladder of law has no top and no bottom
> Stared at the person who killed for no reason
> Who just happened to be feeling that way without warning

And he spoke through his cloak, most deep and distin-
    guished
And handed out strongly, for penalty and repentance
William Zanzinger with a six-month sentence—

—with those last words staggered, "a six, month, sentence," the way the words are spoken carrying at once disbelief at the fact and disbelief that it would have turned
out any other way. When you listen, it's as if the singer can
barely expel the last word. It breaks and stumbles in his
mouth, as if he will never not be shocked. "Bury the rag
deep in your face / Now's the time for your tears," the song's
last chorus ended, but for power and dominion as those
qualities gathered in the music, in the air, in the public
square, they didn't touch the tone of voice on the last four
words of the last verse. "One of the best songs Bob has
ever written," Paul Nelson wrote in his three-stars-out-of-
five review of *The Times They Are A-Changin'* in *Little Sandy
Review* (along with two stars each for *Joan Baez in Concert*
and *Joan Baez in Concert, Part 2*), but nearly twenty years
later, watching Dylan perform the song at the start of his
Rolling Thunder odyssey, Nelson, who died in 2006 at seventy, heard much more: "a mixture of rage and severity"
that "when combined with the near-brutal austerity of his
singing, somehow suggests a cosmic system of justice so
infinite and implacable that the courts and judges of this
world seem worth taking seriously only until the purge
comes. I can feel it breathing down my neck right now."

As we listened in 2019, we heard both the play the song

staged and how the drama was fashioned—how the scene was set, the props arranged, how the lighting fell, how the company was cast. We heard the ambition to write a history that will last as long as *Antigone.* And we could hear the way the song was made to write its own history.

Thirty-four years after Bob Dylan wrote the song, in 1997, the Baltimore cop show *Homicide* ran three episodes about the murder of a Haitian maid employed by a rich, African-American Baltimore family; the father, played by James Earl Jones, had shielded his guilty son. Why? Because of William Zantzinger, the Jones character says, and he tells the old story—forgotten as something that was once reported in a newspaper, never forgotten as a play once staged all over the country—tells it in Bob Dylan's words, as if those words are now part of the Constitution, as if a white man's crime should pay for a black man's, an eye for an eye and a tooth for a tooth—even if in both cases the eyes that close are those of a poor black woman. "'In the courtroom of honor, the judge pounded his gavel, to show that all's equal and the courts are on the level,'" Jones explained to Andre Braugher's homicide detective, the Braugher character too young to remember, Jones speaking in a way that was at once ordinary and oracular, so that it was impossible to read his tone: "'And that the ladder of law has no top and no bottom.'" But the law had a top and a bottom for William Zantzinger and Hattie Carroll, Jones was saying: *Doesn't my boy deserve the same?* A song that once seemed so clear, that sounded as if its words might be chiseled over some courthouse door, now seemed to make no sense at all. The song was writing history, rewriting it, unwriting it—the song, as it played inside *Homicide,* as the plot changed and new actors took their places, was unwriting itself, and writing itself again, for the next theater.

But that was from a time when music and politics were locked together—when so often they spoke the same languages—and as songs from that time traveled down the years, the lock held. To go to a song from a time when that lock had long since been broken—to Laurie Anderson's "O Superman," from 1981—is to enter a very different theater. It wasn't exactly a theater Bob Dylan would ever play, even though you could just make out chalked lyrics from "The Lonesome Death of Hattie Carroll" on support beams and on the backs of floorboards, if you had time to look.

In 1981 Bob Dylan was two years into his new life as a fundamentalist preacher, seeking converts, damning unbelievers. "I told you 'The Times They Are A-Changin''" and they did," he said from the stage in Albuquerque at the start, in 1979. "I said the answer was 'Blowin' in the Wind' and it was. I'm telling you now that Jesus is coming back, and He is!—and there is no other way of salvation." He sounded less like a prophet than Peter Popoff of Peter Popoff Ministries and the most undeniable toupee in the history of Western civilization pitching his Miracle Spring Water on MSNBC as people tearfully testified how checks for tens of thousands appeared in their mailboxes: "God has so much more for you than you're getting!" It was two years into the Margaret Thatcher years in the U.K., and the very beginning of the Reagan years in the United States. This was not a transitional period. It was a transformational era that would alter the rules and the language of politics. Within a few years, what had been a shared language of possibilities changed irrevocably. Certain things—the idea of community, of the public square, of the value or even the existence of civic virtue, of the idea that members of a society were held together in a web of rights and obligations, of a shared history and a shared future—became impossible to talk about. Now society was divided between those who were worthy and those who weren't—for that matter, as Margaret Thatcher so famously put it, there was no such thing as society, only "individuals and families." You were on your own. You and your neighbor owed each other nothing, not even the obligation to greet each other in the morning, or the right to expect that if you found yourselves in mutual jeopardy you would help each other. And the artistic corollary was that no artist could expect, by the rules and language of pop music, that anyone had any reason to be interested in what she had to say. Laurie Anderson started from this premise: a world completely different from the one in which, so long before, "The Lonesome Death of Hattie Carroll" could sound like a gong that would echo forever. That was her subject.

With the landslide victory in 1980 of Ronald Reagan, for decades the tribune of a revanchist, brutalist right-wing vision of the world, the United States had made a new decision about what its citizens would do with their shared space and time, and Anderson was adding her voice to the national conversation—but as she told me when we talked about "O Superman" in February 2019, the beginnings of the story went back to a period much closer to the time when Bob Dylan wrote his song.

It went back to an artistic commune called ZBS Media—or, really, it went back to a 1950s TV show called *The Millionaire,* where every week the billionaire John Beresford Tipton, his voice heard but his face never seen, gave some unsuspecting person a million dollars. His emissary would show up on someone's doorstep and hand the beneficiary a check—and then the billionaire would watch, like a god, like a peeping tom, to see how the money changed the person's life—sometimes, how it ruined it.

As Anderson tells the story, it began one day in the late 1960s—when there was so much money floating around the economy that people with too much of it and crazy schemes about what to do with it were popping up all over the place. At that time, a disc jockey in New Orleans—the kind of DJ who played records on the radio, not in a club—got a call from a man who said, *I have a million dollars I want to give you, to start an audio collective.* It wasn't a joke. The DJ agreed and the money arrived. The DJ recruited eight or nine others, including the Canadian music producer Roma Baran. In the early seventies they found a property in Fort Edward, New York, a small town on the Hudson River. They built a recording studio. "It went through every sphere a commune goes through," Anderson says. "Music—jazz—drugs, sex. Long involved radio plays. One guy is still there—the commune broke up when the babies started to come."

One day in 1973, when Anderson was in her mid-twenties, a former Egyptology student from Chicago who played around with a violin in the insular New York City performance-art scene—at one point, she played it on the street, sometimes standing on a block of ice, until it melted and she walked on—she got a letter. "I'd been hitchhiking to the North Pole. I didn't make it. But when I got back to my apartment on Avenue C"—the lower Lower East Side in Manhattan, Alphabet City, where in the early seventies the economy essentially consisted of drugs, prostitution, burglary, and markets in stolen goods—she found her building boarded up, and everything she had gone. But mail was still being delivered, and what Anderson found was an invitation to serve as an artist in residence at something called ZBS. Effectively homeless, she called. "Can I come now?" "Now?" So she went.

She began working with Baran and the sound designer Bob Bielecki. "I had lots of songs," she says; back in New York, she began taking them into tiny clubs, playing them in bits and pieces. A friend who worked for Warner Bros., at the time the coolest company in the music business, urged her to record them. "I had no interest in making records," Anderson says. Some years ago, in an onstage conversation, she put it more bluntly. "I wasn't interested in having my music on the radio," she said. "I think popular culture is *stupid.*" I said that to me that was like saying the air is stupid, but she wasn't impressed.

She was working with art galleries. She was working in Europe with people associated with the opera director Philip Glass—with the conductor Dennis Russell Davies and the black American tenor Charles Holland. After working as a jazz singer with Fletcher Henderson and Benny Carter in the 1930s, Holland had made his solo debut with a recital in New York in 1940, but as with the character Jonah Strom in Richard Power's epic novel *The Time of Our Singing* ("whose voice," as Jonah Strom's brother describes it, "could make heads of state repent"), a character perhaps inspired by Holland, racism poisoned Holland's career, and he left the country. Holland performed in Paris, London, across Europe, in *Faust,* Verdi's *Otello, The Magic Flute.* He was seventy-seven when he died in 1987 at his home in the Netherlands. "They were expats," Anderson says of Davies and Holland in the mid-seventies. "I considered myself an expat too."

Above all else, Anderson was struck by Holland's performances of the Paris composer Jules Massenet's 1885 "O Souverain, O Juge, O Père," from Massenet's opera *Le Cid,* which she first heard Holland sing in Berkeley in 1977. "Holland killed with that song," Anderson says. "It was one of the most beautiful songs I ever heard. And I thought—I'm going to do an American version. I'm going to write a song for the United States"—not about, but for. "'O Souverain' is a prayer," she says, "and 'O Superman' is a prayer, too." "O Superman—oh judge—oh Mom and Dad," she began, with a lift in the second word, "O Su-*per*man," to let the music in from the start.

As with other songs, Anderson began working it out in clubs. Roma Baran insisted they record it. Anderson had a tiny studio next to an elevator—whatever she recorded had elevator noise seeping in, and it was the same with "O Superman." "If you make it really loud," Anderson says today, "you can hear the elevator in it. You can hear the conversations people were having in the elevator."

"All your work is on the one," Roma Baran complained. "I don't like downbeats," Anderson says—"That doesn't mean I don't want a beat." In "O Superman," a constant loop of a breath—a clipped, staccato *ah ah ah*—is the song's implacable beat, depending on how you hear it the threatening beat, the tyrannical beat, in its way undermining the song, destroying it, less orchestrating everything else in the song than denying its claim to make its own sound, or to mean anything at all.

Anderson had a $500 grant from the National Endowment for the Arts—one of Ronald Reagan's first acts as president was an attempt to eliminate the agency altogether. Anderson used some of the money to have five hundred 45s made. If she got a request, she says, "I'd pack up a copy, walk to the post office, put it in the mail." She heard from Bob George, who had just started a project called the ARChive of Contemporary Music—a collection that now includes more than five million albums, singles, and everything else related to pop music. He had also started his own record label, One Ten Records, named after his apartment at 110 Chambers Street. He pressed five thousand copies, which the London independent label

Rough Trade took on. They disappeared. Warner Bros. came knocking again. The DJ John Peel—the most powerful tastemaker in the U.K.—began playing the record. He asked for more copies. "How many?" Anderson remembers asking. "He said, ten thousand. And ten thousand next week." Anderson said yes to Warner Bros. In October they shipped 125,000 copies to the U.K. and within two weeks it was number 2 on the charts.

The song never had that kind of presence in the United States. If you heard it on the radio, on some so-called free form station, it was usually around midnight. But Anderson was already performing the song in public.

In the fall of 1981, in San Francisco, with William Burroughs as her opening act, Anderson took the stage in a music space called the Cinema, a converted movie theater, in a black satin jacket, black shirt, black tie, black pants, her eyes made up like someone out of the Village of the Damned, her hair chopped and spiked into a punk do. The place was packed; she immediately defused the expectations of the audience with a bit of rambling, deadpan patter. She mimed with a neon violin and set a few tapes rolling to no apparent purpose. The crowd had greeted her as a priest of high art; having broken that promise, she faded into "O Superman."

Playing a Farfisa organ, filtering and electronically distorting her voice against that never changing *ah ah ah,* she set comedy against fear. Much of her work that night was academic deconstruction; here the object of deconstruction, the object of destruction, was the United States itself.

If it was a prayer for the United States, it could have been a prayer that the United States would end.

It begins as if in a fifties TV family sitcom—instead of Massenet's reverent "Oh Father," it's that "Oh Mom and Dad," uttered in the flat American voice of a bored teenage girl. There's a modern, 1980s opening, with the then-new leave-a-message instructions of an answering machine. There's Mother checking in—"Are you coming home?"— and then an anonymous voice: the voice, you come to think soon enough, of the national fortune-teller.

"Well, you don't know me," the creamy voice says, at once spectral and a body itself, untouchable and physical. "But I know you"—and if you think you're now listening to the government, eavesdropping on your every word and thought, in the same instant you hear the voice of a stalker, a rapist, or even your own subconscious mind. "But I know you"—the sound carries entitlement, as if the entity behind the voice, inside the voice, has rights to you that you've never even thought of. The voice goes on—now a salesman, cold-calling to sell you earthquake insurance, now a prophet, delivering a warning, if you'll just keep listening to the message. A feeling of tension is beginning to close in.

"You don't know me/But I know you/And I've got a message/To give to you/Here come the planes . . . " The last word is drawn out electronically, to give you time to think about it. Are these the planes that anyone of Laurie Anderson's generation, and mine, practiced hiding from under our desks in school, the Russian planes loaded with atom bombs, the planes we heard as we lay in our beds at night, wondering if this was it, if this was the one, the planes that never did arrive? In the Cinema that night in 1981, the line was so loaded with portent I found myself involuntarily glancing up at the ceiling, as if the planes were going to come right through the roof.

All of that goes in and out of the song in a split second, part of the common memory the song is drawing from. The drawn-out word carries over into the next movement, and the voice goes on, not pressing any harder, but feeling more dangerous: "So you'd better get ready / Ready to go / You can come as you are / But pay as you go"—the last two lines as American a homily as anyone has ever composed.

The voice creates the sense that one has incurred a debt without knowing it, and that one must now make the debt good, without knowing what you have to pay, let alone why. It's the Carter Family's "Worried Man Blues," from 1930, in the ditch of the Great Depression, all over again: "I went across the river, I lay down to sleep / I went across the river, I lay down to sleep / When I woke up, the shackles on my feet." As it was that night in San Francisco, as it is any time you play the record, the moment is absolutely terrifying. Then there's that prim little lilt, the voice sadistically laughing over how scared you might be: "They're American planes / Made in America / Smoking"— as planes still were in 1981—"or *Non*-smoking."

The woman whose machine has picked up the call now picks up the phone herself, but the voice continues with its riddles as if there's been no interruption: "Neither snow nor rain, nor gloom of night, shall stay these carriers, from the swift completion, of their appointed rounds." The voice is gentle, ageless, summoning up old catchphrases, old certainties—in this case, the motto running across the face of any central post office in any American big city— but these couriers, you knew in 1981, you hear whenever you listen, are not delivering the mail. There isn't a note, a word, an inflection that doesn't fulfill its intent to advance the awful mood of the performance—in moments you can almost hear Anderson crouching behind a line, hear her back off from the line even as she delivers it.

The song drifts away. The voice departs, and the woman is left to make peace with its echo, to make sense of it. She half-becomes the specter that was speaking to her and at the same time desperately tries to hold onto the person she was when she first turned on the machine. She gives a speech, or a sermon:

> When love is gone
> There's always justice
> And when justice is gone
> There's always force

There's a pause, as if nothing could follow this—

> And when force is gone
> There's always Mom (Hi Mom!)

"So hold me now," the singer commands, but it's as if the command is coming from far away, from someone else, from the judge who appeared in the first line of the song. As the music begins to sweep up the singer, to make a vortex, like the vortex that swallowed the *Pequod* at the end of *Moby-Dick,* the singer wraps her own arms around herself, as if she is her own mother, her own nation: "In your long arms . . . Your petrochemical arms," the second word rushed over its syllables, " . . . your electronic arms," the second word broken up as if its four syllables are about to break off from each other, " . . . your military arms."

Was "O Superman" as finished a vision of America as it seemed to be? Was it just another would-be pop star looking for her first hit? If the country had ever heard the song on the radio every day, as in 1981 people in the U.K. were hearing it, heard it for years, appearing when you weren't expecting it, making your day stop, asking all the questions the song didn't answer, heard it waking up, driving the car, heard it without warning, without intent, then, I thought in 1981, we might find out how strong the song really was.

We found out. In a manner almost too literal to think about, as if the song had been a plan—as if the song, as it opened into the future, had always had room for more verses—the plan was put into play. It was one thing to imagine what the planes in that "Here come the planes" really were; it was something else to be told, and not by the singer. It was something else to see the planes arrive, and, by destroying symbols of a nation's power, to symbolically enact the destruction of the nation itself.

On September 19, 2001, eight days after the terrorist attacks on the World Trade Center and the Pentagon, with a fourth plane headed to the Capitol in Washington, D.C., brought down by its own passengers, Anderson took the stage at Town Hall in New York City, where thirty-eight years before Bob Dylan had performed "With God on Our Side" and "Masters of War." She delivered a little sermon on heart and soul, and then made her way through many songs until she reached "O Superman." It became clear, even as the other songs came into sharper focus than they ever had before, that this was her "Gimmie Shelter," her "Anarchy in the UK," her "Sugar, Sugar," her "Hey Ya"—it's the end of the world, and it's catchy. Like *Scream* stalking Drew Barrymore, it was always scary; it was always cute. But now, this night, instead of looking into the future, sensing a drama and a fate the country implicitly contained within itself, the song was looking back on a future that had already taken place.

You had to wonder: who, *what* wrote "Here come the planes / They're American planes / Made in America / Smoking—or Non-Smoking"—and how did Anderson speak those lines after it had been revealed that that "Smoking" was the answer the song had always contained?

Here, for a moment, the notions of art and politics, speaking the same language, or speaking in foreign tongues, lost their meaning. Art said what politics could not say; politics didn't listen. The song floated off. There is no way to know what events it still contains. In a certain way, the song itself, not just that *ah ah ah,* was always there—waiting to be found by a certain artist, present before she was, present when she's gone. That may be beyond politics, beyond art, beyond music.

It was only three years later that I went to the Oakland Coliseum to see Fleetwood Mac. It was a good show. It was clear they'd never escape *Rumours,* but the new songs didn't sound new and the old songs didn't sound old. "Someone once said, 'When love is gone, there's always justice, and when justice is gone, there's always force,'" Lindsey Buckingham said, introducing his song "Peacekeeper," a middle-of-the-night meditation on the Iraq War, then only into its second year. It was as if the lines from a pop hit from merely twenty-three years before, still under copyright, its author still collecting royalties, were now nothing more than lines from an old folk song.

That is where, as in that episode of *Homicide,* James Earl Jones quoting lines as if they were common coin, that needed no further introduction, "O Superman" met "The Lonesome Death of Hattie Carroll." It was strange and somehow thrilling to see, as the years went on, songs come loose from their authors. It was humbling to hear how songs not only mark history, or even make it, but become part of its fabric, or part of the flag—for whatever, you can hear the songs saying, one in rage and disgust, the other from a calm distance, that might be worth.

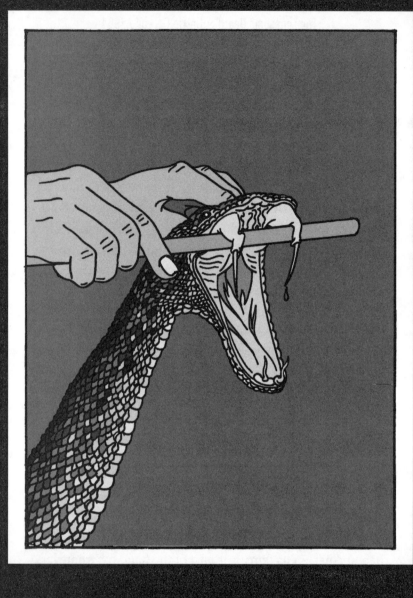

AIN'T TALKIN'

2006

Following the measured cadence, one foot in front of the other and not a step without thinking it through, you can picture a figure crossing a Great War battlefield, the ruins of trenches and barbed wire, the gassy smell of garlic still in the air, land mines everywhere underfoot. When you begin to follow the story the singer is telling, the sky lightens, there's more freedom of movement, but that undertow, the physical sense, the factual knowledge, that you're walking on bodies, is still there.

The song opens on piano, guitar, violin, elegant, shimmering like those velvet-drapes opening credits to any given forties film noir, suspending the song in the air. Then, "As I walked out"—an opening from a thousand songs into a thousand more. You open a door, the world is at your feet. There's an echo from Dylan's own "As I Went Out One Morning," from *John Wesley Harding* almost forty years before, as paradoxical a song as he ever wrote, a three-way waltz between the singer, Tom Paine, and "the fairest damsel / That ever did walk in chains," she beckoning the singer to escape with her to the South, where men and women lived in chains, but also the musical source of freedom in America, then Tom Paine apologizing "for what she's done," a faraway, half-remembered cloudiness in the melody that seems to float just above the people talking in the song. Yet what's odd about the instrumental opening of "Ain't Talkin'"—something you don't think about, you don't even hear, but that travels through the song, an unconscious perception that puts a haze over everything described—is that the musicians are playing an ending, not a beginning. That's the elegance: the elegance of closing a door.

The singer walks out not one morning, but one night. Into what he calls the mystic garden. "I was passing by yon cool crystal fountain," he says flatly, a memory already forming. Someone hits him from behind.

From that point on it's a wandering. Not the folk singer's nirvana—never caught better than in the Folksmen's "Never Did No Wanderin'," from Christopher Guest's horribly embarrassing Folk World movie *A Mighty Wind,* a sadistically accurate Kingston Trio knockdown ("Never heard the whistle of a southbound freight/Or the singing of its drivin' wheel") that's stirring in spite of itself.* It was not a secret that "Ain't Talkin'" traces its path with

* The Folksmen were a fake group made up of Harry Shearer (bass fiddle), Michael McKean (guitar), and Guest (mandolin and banjo). The movie was successful enough that not only did they go on tour, in 2001 they performed at a concert organized by the late Hal Willner to celebrate Harry Smith's *Anthology of American Folk Music,* alongside, among others, David

lines from Ovid. There is "If I catch my opponents ever sleeping, I'll just slaughter them where they lay" and the lovely, modestly final "In the last outback, at the world's end," the song's last line. There is Ovid's "I practice terms long abandoned," lifted past itself with Dylan's stone-faced delivery of the unnerving "I practice a faith that's been long abandoned"—unnerving because part of you wants to know what it is and another part is afraid to find out. But what brings a listener into the language the song speaks is a rhyme so embedded in American English you can imagine John Smith mouthing it to himself as he took his first steps into Virginia: "Ain't talkin', just walkin'."

It's coded. The gospel commonplace "Your walk talks louder than your talk talks" migrates from the Rev. Dr. Adam Clayton Powell's sermon in the Abyssinian Baptist Church on 138th Street in Harlem in 1929 over to 125th and a dope dealer bracing his client: "Don't let your mouth write a check your ass can't cash." "Walk Talk is ready to make an album called Hello Hello and we need your help to make it happen!" a band posted in Indiegogo in 2018. "These songs are made to celebrate the goodness of the groove. They are made for the lover in you. This is our melodic gift to everyone from anywhere." It comes from the dust and it's gone with the wind, just like a Big Gulp

---

Thomas, Elvis Costello, Kate and Anna McGarrigle, Marianne Faithfull, and Garth and Maud Hudson. Thomas sang Henry Thomas's 1929 "Fishing Blues." Faithfull did Blind Willie Johnson's 1930 "John the Revelator." Costello did Dick Justice's 1932 "Henry Lee." The Folksmen came up with Irene Cara's 1983 "Flashdance . . . What a Feeling," on acoustic guitars.

cup on the side of a road. Walk, talk: it's not a phrase, it's a gesture, a posture, a way of carrying yourself that speaks of foreboding and escape. It's so embedded in the rhythms of American experience, so you-can't-have-one-without-the-other, that when in 1926, in Chicago, the twenty-four-year-old Homer Quincy Smith of Florence, Alabama, sounding as if he'd already lived and died ten times over, recorded the most frightening gospel record anyone has ever found—a plea for safe passage through life, Smith's huge voice riding a high, wavering organ sound that feels as if it comes not from his accompanist's hands but from Smith's own forehead, Smith's voice so deserving and bereft that he makes you understand how what he wants is more than anyone could ever rightly ask for—

I want Jesus
To walk with me
I want Jesus
To walk with me
All along my
Pilgrim journey
I want Jesus
To walk with me

—Paramount Records titled it "I Want Jesus to Talk with Me." They just had to. The American language titled it.

Walk and talk: Bob Dylan or anyone else would have heard the words in lockstep in too many songs to remember. But there is one he wouldn't have forgotten in 2006, when "Ain't Talkin'" closed his album *Modern Times,* his twenty-ninth album and his first to reach number one in thirty years. And along with his own "Going, Going, Gone," from 1974, "A Hard Rain's A-Gonna Fall" (1963), "Tangled Up in Blue" (1975), "New Danville Girl" (1984), "Highlands" (1997), and "Sugar Baby" (2001), one more song hangs over "Ain't Talkin'" as a challenge, a singer inspired and countered by his own past, what he heard and what he wrote: can you match this?

"Producer said, 'Jack, we need one more song,'" the late-fifties Top 40 hitmaker Jack Scott said from a stage in his hometown of Detroit in 2014, an electric guitar in his hands. "I said, 'Well, I had one, but I didn't finish it.' He said, 'Well, why don't you try to do a little bit of it, and, ah, we'll see where it goes.' So I told the vocal group, 'Guys, just do a little bit of a "doo-ya doo-ya doo-wop" thing or something, and we'll see what it sounds like.' Two weeks later he calls me and tells me 'You got a new song out' and I said, 'What's that?' and he says, 'The song you didn't finish, "The Way I Walk."'"

Scott had had top 10 hits—the slow-dance ballad "My True Love" and "Goodbye Baby," his irresistibly stutter-step follow-up to Jody Reynolds's "Endless Sleep," in 1958—and would have two more, the country-tone "What in the World's Come Over You" and the weeper-with-female-chorus "Burning Bridges" in 1960. In 1959 "The Way I Walk" reached only number 35, but it was indelible then, sinking right into your breastbone, and it's the legacy that Scott, who died in 2019 at eighty-three, left behind.

He had slicked-back hair and a sneering mouth. He looked as much like Mick Jones of the Clash as James Dean—which only speaks of the visual highway of the rock 'n' roll look. The song opened cold, the singer staring you in the face, the Elvis of "Baby, Let's Play House," on his own, nothing but his pompadour and his acoustic guitar, a click on the drummer's sticks, as coolly punk as anything the fifties ever turned up. "The way I walk is just the way I walk," Scott says, as if it could have ever been different. "The way I talk is just the way I talk." I can't help but think of it all going back to whoever it was that first took up the story that Homer would put his name on: *Enter Achilles. "The way I walk is just the way I walk."* Until it wasn't.

The opening really is that stark. It matches Tennessee Ernie Ford's "When you see me coming, better step aside" and slips past it because it doesn't need a pause, and because it's modest, not a threat, merely what anyone would like to think of themselves. There's menace in the voice, worn lightly, a spring in the steps of the words as they follow one after another, each slightly in its own gravity, the sense of cadence that opens "Ain't Talkin'," here a matter of Jack Scott strolling out of his house and taking his first steps into the street, but also back in his bathroom combing his hair in the mirror. The Chantones come in after a second verse, with a light, white *doot-doot, doot-doot,* someone with a deeper voice doing *Yip yip, yip yip,* the lightest drums, a saxophone solo, a sliding, high-note guitar solo, with Scott offering laconic hipster commentary: "That's about right." "Yeahhhh." It's doo-wop rockabilly, a perfect record, maybe because what you want most of all is for Scott to end it as unaccompanied as he was at the start, without buddies, without landscape, and he doesn't. It leaves you absolutely needing to hear it again.

So as "Ain't Talkin'" opens, it's not only the Roman poet Ovid exiled by Augustus to the Black Sea in the first years of the first millennium, it's also a cool cat from the Motor City who once had songs on the radio, now an old man, walking down the street, the evening darker than he'd like, when someone hits him from behind, and then the singer isn't Jack Scott anymore. Now four lines of thought follow four lines that are not quite narrative, almost telling a story but snatching it away as soon as it comes into focus, as will happen throughout the whole arc of the song, across seventeen verses over nearly nine minutes, the likes of "Well, the whole world is filled with speculation / The whole wide world which people say is round / They will tear your mind away from contemplation / They will jump on your misfortune when you're down" giving way to "Ain't talkin', just walkin' / Eating hog-eyed grease in a hog-eyed town / Heart burnin', still yearnin' / Someday you'll be glad to have me around."

In its slow, trudging pace, the terrain the song covers in its most vivid moments is as American as the way Jack Scott states his case—you're more likely to find hog-eyed grease at a barbeque joint on Eight Mile Road in Detroit than anywhere around the Black Sea—asking for no more and giving no less than two people encountering each other at opposite ends of a bridge over a creek. As D. H.

125

Lawrence put it at the end of a chapter on Fenimore Cooper in *Studies in Classic American Literature:*

> I am I. Here I am. Where are you?
> Ah, there you are! Now, damn the consequences, we have met.
> That's my idea of democracy, if you want to call it an idea.

I think that what might draw anyone to play "Ain't Talkin'" over and over is the wish to hear it begin, again and again. To reexperience the opening of the song, the opening into the song, just as, in 1959, a Jack Scott fan could have lifted the tone arm up off the 45 of "The Way I Walk," once he or she had heard the whole thing, to remaster the recording to its first seven seconds, repeated until the groove ran out, the girl or the boy knowing that the whole song is there, just as the beginning of "Ain't Talkin'," once you know the song, can feel as if it contains everything that follows. If what follows weren't so softly inflamed, so driven by resentment and hatred and vengeance and regret and the wish to bury it all in some kind of cynical peace of mind—that is the story the song tells—then everything after the beginning might feel redundant. And maybe it is.

A theme is stated on Dylan's piano and the guitar of his road-band regular Stu Kimball, but the sound they make is single, as if it's one instrument feeding back on itself; you might just barely catch the violin from Donnie Herron, also from Dylan's band, its sound a thin buzz, as if it too were feedback, the instruments producing their own music, evading whatever the intentions of the players might be. The whole is deliberate and slow, as if there couldn't possibly be any other way to begin this song, whatever it is. It suggests a complete world, a world made of morals and emotion, the emotions that fester, then rise up, when morals are broken. As you sense the world the theme makes, you hear in the music that that world is also being judged, and that the judgment isn't final. All of that is happening.

After twelve seconds the theme repeats, this time with the violin much stronger, hovering over the music, as if looking for a way out. Each instrument makes a tone, and the tones shift against each other, like plates on the side of a ship if they moved with the shape of the water. You might begin to hear a particular song playing inside of the hesitations and doubts, inside the sense that this is all preordained: Robert Johnson's "Come On in My Kitchen," from seventy years before. That song was about stillness, about stilling life: a musical progression, one sound following another, that carried its own rest. "Can't you hear the wind howl?" Johnson mutters under his breath in the middle of the song in 1936, twice, making you lean forward to hear what he's saying, and it can seem like mere chance that you can. The sound is that intimate, as if a makeshift recording setup in a room in the Gunter Hotel in San Antonio were a Greenwood juke joint with a tin roof after everyone else has gone home. With "Ain't Talkin'" the first theme takes one step back for every step forward, resisting itself, resisting the notion, even the need, that anything might follow.

When the theme shifts to a cantering pace just before Dylan sings the first line, it's a shift to a more predictable rhythm. The weight in the music lifts. It's four seconds, a little more, but the opening credits are gone, the establishing shot is in place, and when the singer says, in a rough but matter-of-fact voice, "As I walked out tonight in the mystic garden," it can seem as if you've already heard it, as if he's saying it for the second time. As the song moves forward it absolutely doesn't want to.

"Someone hit me from behind." From performance to performance, from the first time Dylan played the song, in New York in 2006, to the last, so far, in Rome seven years later, that moment is dramatized distantly, or as a curse, with fury or fatigue. It's not a detective story. There's no attempt to track down whoever it was, only an unfocused loathing, a condemnation of the world, all seen in an instant: "As I walked out tonight." Tonight: everything that's described, seen, thought, is happening as the blow is struck and the singer falls, even as he falls, before he hits the ground. It's a fever dream, and when he comes to fifteen verses later there's a woman in the garden, the night has changed to day, he senses that she's looking for a sign, but there's nothing to see: "Excuse me, ma'am, I beg your pardon / There's no one here, the gardener is gone." God—the first gardener, in Eden, the gardener Jesus calls when in John 15:1 he says, "I am the true vine, and my Father is the gardener," has left this place, and left those who remain to silence. It calls back Fairport Convention's wordless, almost motionless 1967 "The Lord Is in This Place," a version of Blind Willie Johnson's 1927 "Dark Was the Night—Cold Was the Ground"—which despite its title dramatized precisely the same abandonment.

Like "A Hard Rain's A-Gonna Fall," "Ain't Talkin'" opens up into a quest. In the first song a young man leaves home to travel the world and, drawing on the imagery of the ancient British ballad "Nottamun Town," where not a soul would look up and not a soul would look down and ten thousand was drownded that never was born, returns with a tale just as shaken and absurd. In Dylan's song people try to speak, but they can't: "I saw ten thousand talkers whose tongues were all broken." Even if they could speak it wouldn't matter: "I heard ten thousand whisperin' and nobody listenin'." The singer is shocked, and sparked to action. He takes on the mantle of Amos, raising the specter of the rain God sent to cleanse the world, drowning all those who had proved themselves unworthy of being born. After each verse describing a world in ruins, the chorus swings the mirror back on the singer, on the listener: "And it's a hard, it's a hard, it's a hard, it's a hard—It's a hard rain, 's a-gonna fall." Every time Dylan has sung the song, from a Carnegie Chapter Hall hootenanny on September 22, 1962, to the soulful performance he gave at George Harrison's Concert for Bangladesh in 1971, repeating the last line three times as he ended the song, when he's raised and stretched his voice, it becomes a bird he can barely catch. Finally he will return to the world, no longer as a prophet but as an avatar, climbing the ramparts of the song to save the world: "And I'll tell it and think it and speak it and breathe it / And reflect it from the mountain so all souls can see it." The sense of triumph is overwhelming. He started out as a boy, "my blue-eyed son, my darling young one," but now he's a man. Power and dominion over the spirits? He claims that power and that dominion because he's made the journey, because he's earned it.

Like "The Lonesome Death of Hattie Carroll," the song is a staircase, but more deliberately, without jeopardy in every step. Each staggered line of testimony—

I saw a highway of diamonds with nobody on it
I saw a black branch with blood that kept drippin'
I saw a roomful of men with their hammers a-bleedin'
I saw a white ladder all covered with water

—is a step. Each recurring question—"Where have you been?" "What did you see?" "What did you hear?" "Who did you meet?," all questions from the Child ballad "Lord Randall": "Where ha'e you been?" "Wha met ye there?" "What did she give you?"—is a landing. It's a structure the musicologist Steven Rings traces to a prison recording made by the father-and-son song collectors John Lomax (1867–1948) and Alan Lomax (1915–2007) in 1936, Lemuel Jones's lining-out "It's Hard on We Po' Farmers," for Dylan's chorus, and Roy Orbison's 1961 "Running Scared" for the climb of the verses. As I was lucky to do one afternoon at a conference in Tulsa in 2019, you only have to hear Rings make the argument and play the songs to realize he's right. "I moved the dial up and down and Roy Orbison's voice came blasting out of the small speakers. His new song, 'Running Scared,' exploded into the room," Dylan set his Roy Orbison scene in *Chronicles*. "He sang like a professional criminal. Typically, he'd start out in some low, barely audible range, stay there a while and then astonishingly slip into histrionics. His voice could jar a corpse." Dylan couldn't even imagine touching Orbison's three-octave range, but Orbison gave him ambition. "He sounded like he was singing from an Olympian mountain-top"—Orbison let Dylan see through those eyes.

"Running Scared" is a heroic song. So is "A Hard Rain's A-Gonna Fall"—not for the tale it tells but for the fact that it was written at all. "Every line in that really is another song," Dylan told Studs Terkel in 1963. "Could be used as a whole song, every single line. I wrote that when I didn't know how many other songs I could write. That was during October of last year and I remember sitting up all night with a bunch of people someplace. I wanted to get the most down that I knew about into one song, so I wrote that. It was during the Cuba trouble, that blockade, I guess is the word." It wasn't—as with that Carnegie Chapter Hall show, the Cuban missile crisis, a standoff that stopped the world in its tracks, began weeks after Dylan first sang the song. But even if the song existed before the event, the event went into the song. "Someone pointed out it was written before the missile crisis," Dylan said to Robert

Hilburn in 2004, "but it doesn't really matter where a song comes from. It just matters where it takes you."

That was how people heard it—including its composer. They were reliving the history they had passed through when they listened, and so, with both the United States and the Soviet Union threatening nuclear war, after the secret negotiations that ended the standoff—the world knew that Nikita Khrushchev withdrew his missiles from Cuba, but not that John F. Kennedy dismantled his missiles in Turkey—that was how Bob Dylan sang it. That was how he sang it during the crisis and after it. History had entered the song, and the song wrote part of that history. You can't help but hear it that way, now, as Dylan performed the song for an after-hours show at the Gaslight sometime in early October of 1962—before the missile crisis, in historical fact, but, listening to the recording that surfaced only long after that fact, also after it. As the verses build on each other, the people in the audience (no tourists, but friends and musicians, there for a session recorded professionally by the sound engineer Richard Alderson, who in 1966 toured with Dylan and the Hawks from Australia to Paris and recorded dozens of the shows), begin to sing the chorus. At first there are only a few, by the end seemingly a whole company, what was at first hesitant now full, loud, embracing, a defiance, a celebration: we are here, we have this song to sing. Where's the capital of the United States? Is it Washington, D.C., or Washington Square in Greenwich Village? The White House or, not two blocks from the statue of Washington on the arch, the Gaslight Café?

It doesn't matter which side of the night that time fell on.

"I guess that was the first three-dimensional song I wrote," Dylan told Terkel. It lasted. In 1973 Bryan Ferry would make it the lead track for *These Foolish Things,* his first solo album away from Roxy Music, an "album of covers of some of my favorite songs," he said in 2021. "I was not an expert on Bob Dylan, but I admired his work and especially his lyrics. 'Hard Rain' was the song I chose and it has lots of words. It's not a love song, but it has plenty of passion. I wanted to make it different from his original simple acoustic guitar version, and the natural way for me to play it was up-tempo on the piano, banging on the keys, and being quite aggressive with the song. John Porter's bass is a really important part of the feel of the track, as is the powerful drumming of Paul Thompson. Eddie Jobson did a great string arrangement, playing all the parts himself. Dr. John's backing singers were passing through town, and they did some wonderful singing on the chorus. We threw in a few sound effects for good measure"— staccato *ha-ha-ha-ha*s for "I saw many people laughing," a wave crashing for "I heard the sound of a wave that could drown the whole world," rain coming down as it the song faded out. It all added to the camp atmosphere around the song ("Is this some kind of joke?" Robbie Robertson, Dylan's guitarist in 1973, said when he heard it)—but if Ferry's singing at first sounded like Bela Lugosi, this was camp without irony, a headlong dive to the bottom of the song's ocean, jerked steps not merely line to line or word to word but within words, a great roar, a way of saying, if you can hear what I'm doing with this song, you'll know there are no limits to what can be done with it, or how far it can go. That for *These Foolish Things* Ferry followed it with, among other "songs from my record collection," Lesley Gore's "It's My Party," the Beach Boys' "Don't Worry Baby," and Elvis Presley's "Baby I Don't Care,"* was his argument that while the song might aim for the heaven of art, its real home was on the charts, which is right where Ferry took it.

And it made sense that it was the song Patti Smith sang when she accepted Dylan's Nobel Prize in his stead. For Dave Van Ronk, even though the few false notes of the song were all too embarrassing ("the 'clown who cried in the alley' always sounded to me like the verbal equivalent of a painting on velvet," he said in his memoir, posthu-

---

* From the 1957 film *Jailhouse Rock*—Elvis sings it standing by a Hollywood swimming pool—"(You're So Square) Baby I Don't Care" was written by Jerry Leiber and Mike Stoller, taking off from the 1947 noir *Out of the Past*. Robert Mitchum is a detective hired to find femme fatale Jane Greer, who has run out on her mobster boyfriend Kirk Douglas after stealing $40,000 and shooting him in the bargain. When he does find her, as Steve Erickson writes, "he can practically see his future down to the last bullet hole." She's allurement as a force of nature. When they're alone and she says, "But I didn't take anything. I didn't take anything . . . won't you believe me?" and Mitchum answers, "Baby, I don't care," you know just how he feels. "Leiber and Stoller didn't think much of my songs," Dylan said in his MusiCares speech, when he settled a lot of scores, verbally slaughtering a lot of enemies where they lay, dead or alive. "They didn't like 'em, but Doc Pomus did. That was all right that they didn't like 'em, because I never liked their songs either. 'Yakety yak, don't talk back.' 'Charlie Brown is a clown.' 'Baby I'm a hog for you.' Novelty songs, not serious. Doc's songs, they were better. 'This Magic Moment.' 'Lonely Avenue.' 'Save the Last Dance for Me.' Those songs broke my heart. I figured I'd rather have his blessings any day than theirs."

mously published in 2005—Van Ronk had died in 2002 at sixty-five), but that was nothing to the territory the song claimed. "I heard him sing that for the first time at one of the hoot nights at the Gaslight," Van Ronk said, "and I could not even talk about it; I just had to leave the club and walk around for a while. It was unlike anything that had come before it, and it was clearly the beginning of a revolution."

All of that is gone when the singer returns to follow the path he laid down more than forty years before. But if again the singer is on a quest, now it's a meander, the quester barely caring what he sees. If he's retracing his steps from that first journey, there's no urgency, no possibility of seeing anything he hasn't seen before. There's only a bitter, sour residue. The singer doesn't want to save the world, he wants to punish it for its failure. "I'll avenge my father's death then I'll step back"—you picture it, it's a scene from a movie. The singer steps up to the killer, hits him from behind, watches as the body falls, moves away, contemplates the tableau like a painter, and leaves: "Ain't talkin', just walkin' / Through the world mysterious and vague," with, as the lines unfold, the word *vague* far more striking than the cheap *mysterious,* all but striking it out. *The world is mysterious, says the singer. Tell me something I don't know, says the person he's talking to. The world is vague. What?*

The words in "Ain't Talkin'" are sometimes so fourth-hand—"This weary world of woe"—that they seem like parodies of sad songs, or self-parodies. Read through the song, or listen to the lyrics, and it can seem as if every strong line—"I'll burn that bridge before you can cross"— is undercut by a weak line: "Heart burnin', still yearnin'." But the song holds infinite fascination, because in the song these are not lines but moments. Each sways back to the other, then swings apart. They're part of a rhythm, a rhythm that won't explain itself, where it began, where it's going.

You can immediately apprehend that "A Hard Rain's A-Gonna Fall" is a great song. I first heard it the week before the March on Washington, in a swampy field at night at Stanford University—heard it from Pete Seeger, who introduced it as by Bob Dylan, who I'd first seen weeks before, coming out to sing during that Joan Baez show in New Jersey. Pete Seeger was an old story that night, Bob Dylan was a story to which I hadn't even caught the title, but even in Seeger's hands the song was the world made fresh. Never mind "Running Scared" and "Nottamun Town": it's a thing in itself, whether it's Bob Dylan trying it out at the Gaslight or placing it between "Duquesne Whistle" and "Pay in Blood" at the Firefly Festival in Dover, Delaware, in 2017, as I write the last time he played the song.

But you can't immediately see what makes "Ain't Talkin'" a great song, one of the most distinctive songs Bob Dylan ever wrote. Or is it sang? Or is it performed? As Dylan has performed "Ain't Talkin'" it has often taken on such a different cast it becomes a different song. The first time, at the City Center in New York, on November 20,

2006, it was like a sermon. At Northrop Auditorium at the University of Minnesota on November 4, 2008, it's as if the singer is remembering something from long ago, but the memory is so troubling it makes you feel that everything it describes is happening as you watch. It becomes a road song, spanning years, even decades; it merges with "Tangled Up in Blue," each song an argument about how to live, how to cross through the world, and each possible.

In Amsterdam at the Heineken Music Hall on April 12, 2009, there's an odd, scratchy opening on the guitar, then a pumping organ. "Someday you'll be *gladdddd* to have me around"—but I'll be long gone before then. It takes shape as a noir western. As it moves on you can see Charles Bronson in *Once Upon a Time in the West,* or Clint Eastwood in *Unforgiven.* Look farther back and you can see Robert Mitchum in *Pursued,* and Robert Ryan in *Day of the Outlaw,* as everything, emotion, obligation, land, the last man, falls.

However "Ain't Talkin'" appears, on record, on a stage, it's not "Running Scared"—the kind of sound Dylan would say "made you want to drive your car over a cliff," which is what Pete Seeger did with "A Hard Rain's A-Gonna Fall." In "Ain't Talkin'" there's a theme, a theme of contemplation, the singer shifting his back against a tree, staring at the sky, and then thoughts begin to take shape, and musically the song follows them. The theme—that opening slide, repeated twice, then taking different shapes but not really fading—pulls the song through its chanted, muttered, declarative singing. It trusts the listener, and the singer trusts himself. "A Hard Rain's A-Gonna Fall" hits you with one line after another like logs piling through a chute. "Ain't Talkin'" drops trap doors. In a miasma where signifiers register less as words than as images, in a movie theater where everything is slightly out of focus, just enough to make you wonder if it's your eyes or the projection that's off, any sound can make you wonder: *Did I hear that? Where are we? What time is it?* With the whole song taking place out of doors, the best lines in the tune seem to come out of nowhere: "I'm eating hog-eyed grease in a hog-eyed town." "Walking with a toothache in my heel." The power of one line, which might be simply in oddness, the way it throws you off, yes, *what* time is it, what century are we in?—"The whole wide world which people say is round"—and the cliché of another—"Walkin' through the cities of the plague"—doesn't matter. Each blow lands with equal weight. And the song is open. You could shuffle the verses and if you kept the first and the last you wouldn't hear the story any differently. That's what Bettye LaVette did with the song on *Things Have Changed,* her 2018 album of Dylan songs, mostly obscure numbers from the 1980s on, insinuating songs often thrown away by Dylan himself on bad albums that wanted a singer who could hear what Dylan himself didn't, or someone who cared about a song when he couldn't be bothered: "Emotionally Yours," "Seeing the Real You at Last," "Don't Fall Apart on Me Tonight," "What Was It You Wanted."

Born Betty Jo Haskins in a town on the western edge of Michigan in 1946, growing up in Detroit, LaVette cut her first record, "My Man—He's a Lovin' Man," in 1962, the same year Bob Dylan cut his, but LaVette made the charts first. "Let Me Down Easy" was the kind of soul record where despair is the lead instrument; it could leave a hole in your heart, but it barely climbed out of the radio in 1965. Her career spiraled so far from itself that she tried prostitution. In *A Woman Like Me,* the autobiography she published in 2012 with David Ritz, she describes her future as she saw it in the 1970s: "I'd walk into a bar, order a drink, and watch a woman in her sixties singing in front of a makeshift band. She was fifty pounds overweight. Her makeup was running. Her clothes were frayed. I could hear that once upon a time her voice had been strong, but now her voice was shot. Her eyes were sad. While she sang, she worked the room, urging the patrons to stuff a dollar bill or two in her bra. Some did, but most didn't. At one point, a guy screamed, 'Let's turn on the jukebox. Anything is better than this bitch!' I wanted to slug the guy. I wanted to cry. I wanted to stop seeing myself in this woman." In the 2000s she recorded with the Drive-By Truckers; she sang "A Change Is Gonna Come" with Jon Bon Jovi for Barack Obama's inaugural celebration. She released an album covering hits by the Beatles, the Animals, the Rolling Stones, topped by a lugubrious version of the Who's "Love Reign O'er Me." None of it was any warning of how she took over Bob Dylan.

"He complains about *everything,*" she said at a show at the Freight and Salvage folk club in Berkeley on April 5, 2019, singing only Dylan songs until her single encore, a shockingly isolated, a cappella version of Sinéad O'Connor's "I Do Not Want What I Haven't Got." "Just like an old woman," LaVette went on. "And I'm an old woman. But when a black woman ages, she can do it in less than nine verses. So I'm finishing Bob Dylan's arguments." That's what she did with "Ain't Talkin'." On record her only instrumentation was the Firey Strings Company, a preternaturally graceful but hard-edged jazz quartet led by the cellist Nioka Workman. "They wrote this string arrangement," LaVette said when she introduced the song in Berkeley. "They came into the studio, they played it once. I told them I wanted them to assume the attitude of naked *banshees* running in the woods, and they did." On stage, with her band behind her, no strings, she traveled through the song. I can listen to her account of it next to Bob Dylan's and I can never tell what she left out, what she moved from one place to another. The commitment the song seems to demand from anyone with the nerve to sing it becomes the subject of the song. Its formal structures, or anyway its original structures, are dice to throw. She seemed to dance through the descent of the song—for it is a descent, someone slowly making her way down a mountain, like Ronald Colman at the end of *Lost Horizon*. As she sang "Ain't Talkin'," as with Dylan it came forth as a long, twisting parable of knowledge and revenge, but with so much drama, such a ceiling of suspense, that you didn't even hear the lines rhyme. She replaced Dylan's tone of resignation, whatever the violence of his words, with defiance. As the men in her band hit their feet in time, walking the song out of its last verse, it was a flood of words at the end of a life. And that was the play Dylan wrote. That was the scene he set for other actors to play.

"Ain't talkin', just walkin'/Carrying a dead man's shield/Heart burnin', still yearnin'/Walking with a tooth-ache in my heel"—that was one verse LaVette didn't sing, maybe because that last line was just too surreal. But it was down-home American surrealism. Black music traveled into white music throughout the nineteenth and twenti-eth centuries, continually merging, separating, merging again—until, when they were both in their seventies, a black soul singer from Detroit could reach the highlight of her career singing the songs of a folk singer from Min-nesota. Because you know Dan:

> Old Dan Tucker was a fine old man
> Washed his face in a frying pan
> Combed his hair with a wagon wheel
> And died with a toothache in his heel
> Get out the way, Old Dan Tucker
> You're too late to get your supper
> Get out the way, Old Dan Tucker
> You're too late to get your supper

* * *

"Once the evening has arrived, I come home and enter my study," Machiavelli wrote in a letter to a friend in 1513.

In the entryway I take off my daytime clothing, covered with mud and dirt, and put on garments that are royal, and suitable for a court. Changed into suitable clothes, I step into the ancient courts of ancient men. Received lovingly by them, I nourish myself on the food that is mine, for which I was born. There I am unashamed to talk with them and ask them the reasons for their actions, and they, with their humanity, answer me.

That's how I see Bob Dylan writing "Ain't Talkin'" —dressed in Ovid's robes, Jack Scott's drape jacket, Old Dan Tucker's cottonfield straw hat, listening to them talk, asking them what they wanted, what they found and what they lost, even asking how it felt to write the lines he was taking from them. "Walkin' with a toothache in my heel" —it's the most obstinate, undefeated line in the whole song. There's a whole map of the country, a slightly different country from the one that shows up on the usual maps, in that line. It would be a mistake to assume there's any road on that map that Bob Dylan, as a historian, as a listener and a scholar, a folk man, doesn't know.

There were three great blackface characters on the minstrel stage before the Civil War. The first was Jim Crow, the crippled, shuffling, dancing stable man, who Thomas Rice, aka Jim Crow Rice, introduced in 1830, with his Jim Crow dance, arms akimbo, heels clicking in the air, a dance that lasted the rest of the century and into the next: "Jump Jim Crow." Then came Rice's Zip Coon, the "learned skolar," the trickster who outfoxes the white man, tall, thin, fast on his feet, playing the fool only to get himself where he wanted to be. Finally he ran for president and won, with the great joke of the notorious racist Congressman Davy Crockett as his vice president—as he celebrated his election at Grant Park in Chicago, quoting Sam Cooke's "A Change Is Gonna Come," Barack Obama was living out an archetype sketched long before. And third was Old Dan Tucker, the stumblebum, the butt of every joke, falling on his face, walking into doors, like the tall tale of the old man who was so absentminded that one cold night he put his pants to bed and folded himself over his chair and froze to death. Bruce Springsteen stomped "Old Dan Tucker" on stages across the country in 2006, with his big Seeger Sessions band, banjo, acoustic guitars, fiddles, drums, bass fiddle, horns, organ, piano, thousands singing along, a Little Sandy Review Chain-Gang Camp nightmare, as first Old Dan died with that toothache in his heel and then got up and fell down again:

Old Dan Tucker come to town
Riding a billy goat, leading a hound
The hound dog barked and billy goat jumped
And landed old Tucker on a stump

The minstrel band leader Dan Emmett, who took credit for "Dixie" and "Turkey in the Straw," though not "Yankee Doodle" and "The Star-Spangled Banner," claimed to have written "Old Dan Tucker" as a teenager, just about the time Rice made "Jump Jim Crow" a national craze, even though Emmett didn't get around to putting the number out in public until the 1840s. "The whole history of these tales can never be traced," Constance Rourke wrote in 1931 in *American Humor: A Study of the National Character,* but she went further than anyone before her. Her book was her affirmation of the three characters in which for her all American culture was rooted: the Yankee pedlar of New England; the backwoodsman of "the Old Southwest," from Missouri to Mississippi, the Florida panhandle to Arkansas; and the black slave in the person of the black-faced white men who made the black man into a childlike buffoon, fit as God made him for mockery and bondage—and, Rourke was certain, through the alchemy of the white man's envy of the black man's freedom from civilization, of the soul wisdom that seemed to hide in japery and animal fables, real black men and women speaking through the blackface, telling their own tall tales. So her Dan Tucker was far older than anything Dan Emmett could have sung from his crib. It was a black folktale—of the sort spirited off the plantations, along with the latest songs and dances, by scouts sent by northern white minstrel performers, who then blacked up and offered them from stages in New York as "Real Plantation Airs and Ditties," just as in the 1920s and '30s northern record companies had scouts traveling the South and bringing back Charley Patton, Son House, Geeshie Wiley, Elvie Thomas, Skip James, Homer Quincy Smith, to make "the Popular Race Record," not to mention scooping up such sometime-blackface folk singers as Frank Hutchison and Clarence Ashley. But this was how white minstrels did Old Dan Tucker lifetimes before:

> Jaybird in de martin's nest.
> To sabe his soul he got no rest.
> Ole Tucker in de foxes' den,
> Out come the young ones nine or ten.
>
> High-hole in de holler tree,
> He poke his bill in for to see,
> De lizard cotch 'im by de snout,
> He call Tucker to pull 'im out.

Rourke followed the animals that appeared in Tucker's tales in their guises as the crow slave, and the bullfrog slave-catcher:

> A bullfrog dressed in soger's close,
> Went in de field to shoot some crows
> De crows smell powder an' fly away,
> De bullfrog mighty mad dat day.

And over time Dan Tucker shape-shifted. "The song and the character in fact underwent those possessive and affectionate changes and additions which meant that many hands have been at work upon them," Rourke wrote.

> Dan Tucker was pictured as a vagabond Negro who was laughed at and scorned by his own kind but who

constantly bobbed up among them with outrageous
small adventures. Since he consorted with the two sag-
est creatures in the animal world of the Negro, the fox
and the jaybird, he was endowed with comical magic;
yet for all this he was an outcast, looming large as he
combed his hair with a wagon wheel and washed his
face in a frying pan, and at last—

as he became "a legendary figure"—

through the transformations of many years changing
from black to white.

And it was this character—white as a Ragshag Bill
from Buffalo chasing the Gold Rush across the continent,
blackfaced on the minstrel stage—who, in a piece that
features centrally in Eric Lott's 1993 study *Love & Theft:
Blackface Minstrelsy & the American Working Class,* a book
Bob Dylan so treasured he named an album after it, putting the title in quotes to signal that he loved the book
and was stealing its name, exploded all over the place.
James Kennard Jr. was an antislavery writer for the *Knickerbocker* who in 1845 wrote a satire, unless he didn't—the
essay was drenched in teasing, but as Lott puts it, Kennard was "mastered by his own irony." "Who Are Our
National Poets?" Kennard asked, and he answered: "Our
negro slaves . . . From that class come the Jim Crows,
the Zip Coons, the Dandy Jims, who have electrified the
world, from them proceed our ONLY TRUE NATIONAL

POETS." And he meant the black American speaking through the blackface mouth:

> The popular song-maker sways the souls of men; the legislator rules only their bodies. The song-maker reigns through love and spiritual affinity; the legislator by brute force. Apply this principle to the American people. Who are our true rulers? The negro poets, to be sure. Do they not set the fashion, and give laws to the public taste? Let one of them, in the swamps of Carolina, compose a new song, and it no sooner reaches the ear of a white amateur, than it is written down, amended (that is, almost spoilt,) printed, and then put upon a course of a rapid dissemination, to cease only within the utmost bounds of Anglo-Saxondom, perhaps of the world.

"This strange piece is absolutely unflinching," Lott writes, and it is so driven that finally you have to think that whatever satire there was in Kennard's essay, it only barely covered what he wanted: in Lott's words, cultural "insurrection." "At no time does the atmosphere of our planet cease to vibrate harmoniously to the immortal songs of the negroes of America," Kennard wrote. "At this present moment," he said of Dan Tucker, "a certain ubiquitous person seems to be in the way of the whole people of these United States simultaneously, (a mere pretender, doubtless, dressed in some cast-off negro clothing,) and any one may hear him told, a hundred times a day, 'Get out ob de way, old Dan Tucker!' "—but, Kennard said, "Dan takes it as an invitation to stay."* "Get out the way, Old Dan Tucker"? *I'm not going anywhere,* he says. *Forget your Zip Coon. Who says I ain't president? I can walk with a toothache in my heel. You can't stop me. Nobody can stop me.* And that's who's walking through "Ain't Talkin'."

Dan Tucker changes from an escaped slave hiding in the woods in Tennessee ("Old Dan Tucker was a fine old man/From his master he would steal," runs a version recorded by John Lomax in Texas in 1939) to a white backwoodsman in the same forest stuck in a tree with the possum he's chasing. He's Bo Diddley's strange, smoky "The

---

* Kennard was born in 1815 in Portsmouth, New Hampshire. In 1834, during a trip to the South, he contracted an infection that in 1837, in Boston, led to the amputation of a leg. By 1841 he had lost the ability to walk, or even, for the most part, move. He was confined to bed, where, A. P. Peabody wrote in the "Memoir" that opens an 1848 collection of Kennard's work, "a frame was fitted to his bed, and on this his . . . writing apparatus was so adjusted, that he could write in a perfectly legible and clear hand, though, except at the very first, only in double columns on a letter-sheet of the ordinary size, the gradual induration of the wrist allowing his fingers only that narrow range of motion," From his bed, he wrote constantly, publishing widely. In 1844 he lost his sight, and then the ability to speak above a whisper, and moved to dictate his work, essays of ten and twenty thousand words, including "Who Are Our National Poets?" He didn't slow down; as he wrote to a cousin, "the more I am deprived of the usual aids, such as eyes, hands, joints, &c., the better I can write, and the easier I can get along in every way. Just shut up your eyes, chop off your hands, and try it. If you have faith and a good amanuensis, my word for it, you will succeed to perfection. I feel in such high spirits about it, that I intend soon to commence writing my life, and expect to become as renowned as Milton, and to get more for my book, to be entitled, 'The Life of an Invalid,' than he did for his Paradise Lost, to say nothing of the fame." He died in 1847.

Great Grandfather," which for a man born Ellas McDaniel in Mississippi in 1928 and recording in New York in 1958 meant his great-grandfather the ex-slave, now in the song an Indian fighter and a frontiersman, a pioneer with a house in the wilderness and twenty-one children, a man who blocked his door with a wagon wheel and "wore the same suit all his life"—"*Allllllll*-a his life," the words drift off into this Dan Tucker's dream of his own claim on the name. Dan Tucker is in the air: one day one person says to another, "You know, I can't make heads or tails of it. I feel like I've got a toothache in my heel." The phrase festers. It travels from state to state. Sometime in the 1850s, a humorist named George H. Derby, writing as John Phoenix in a California newspaper, turns the line into a story, "Tushmaker's Tooth Puller."

A man named Old Byles comes to a Dr. Tushmaker with a tooth he needs pulled. It's so big the dentist has to invent a machine to get it out: "a combination of the lever, pulley, wheel and axle, inclined plane, wedge and screw," with a giant black hook attached to an oversized pair of forceps. The machine fills the room: "Castings were made, and the machine put up in the office, over an iron chair rendered perfectly stationary by iron rods going down into the foundations of the granite building." Tushmaker clamps down and gently turns a lever four feet high: "Old Byles gave a groan and lifted his right leg. Another turn, another groan, and up went the leg again." The tooth is still there. Dr. Tushmaker jerks the lever and Old Byles's head comes off.

There is an autopsy: "The roots of the tooth were found extending down the right side, through the right leg, and turning up in two prongs under the sole of the right foot." "The whole history of these tales can never be traced"—but you can figure that the gist of John Phoenix's tale was floating around long before he put it down, maybe as a plantation folk remedy. "How to ease a toothache with acupressure," one can read on essortment.com. "There are actually two places where pressure can be applied to assist in treating a toothache . . . the point known as 'Chang-Lang' . . . located on the index finger . . . [and] the 'Kroun-Loun' point . . . located between the outer ankle and the Achilles tendon. The point is toward the bottom of the outer ankle, just above the heel, and pressure applied to it should be aimed downward onto the heel bone." And folk remedies turn back into folk fables, which travel unmarked roads, change shape, take new names: "He put his foot in his mouth." The whole history of these tales can never be traced, but it's hard not to hear an echo in "Bob Dylan's 115th Dream." As the old *Oldies But Goodies* albums had it, on his 1965 album *Bringing It All Back Home* it was the last number on the "Jump Side" as opposed to the "Dreamy Side."* Dylan first recorded the song with lifeless folk guitar strumming matching a vocal without a single high or low; it flat-lined. With a band behind him

---

* As on the second in the series, from 1960, with the likes of Jessie Belvin's "Goodnight My Love" and the Nutmegs' "Story Untold" on the Dreamy Side, Joe Turner's "Shake, Rattle and Roll," and the Turbans' "When You Dance" on the Jump.

a day later, it was all snap, Laurel and Hardy chased by a mad bear, the most frantic three-card monte shuffle rock 'n' roll has ever turned up.

Under one Captain Arab—*A*-rab, Dylan makes it, taking a note from Ray Stevens's hit of three years before, "Ahab, the Arab"—Dylan is a sailor on the *Mayflower,* which is also the *Pequod.* He sights land ("Boys, forget the whale," Captain Arab shouts), names it America, and after the captain and the crew are arrested "for carrying harpoons" and he breaks out of jail, he finds himself right in the heart of it. In the heart of modern America, New York City 1965, complete with bums on the Bowery, waiters in drag, banks, parking tickets, scam artists, protest marches, funeral parlors, and telephone booths: "A pay phone was ringing, and it just about blew my mind / When I picked it up and said hello, this foot came through the line."

Modern Times was not Bob Dylan's first number one album in thirty years because it was better than those that came before it. It was number one because it was the crest of a wave that had begun in 1997, when Dylan sent a broken man through a set of songs called *Time Out of Mind.* That record reached number 10 and won the Grammy for Album of the Year. When in high good humor Dylan accepted it ("Everyone worked really hard, even the musicians"), he called up his personal saint ("One time when I was about sixteen or seventeen years old I went to see Buddy Holly play, at the Duluth National Guard Armory, and I was three feet away from him, and he *looked at me,* and, ah, I, just have some kind of feeling that he was, I don't know how or why, but I know he was with us all the time we were making this record"), and quoted "the immortal Robert Johnson: 'The stuff we got will bust your brains out.' " In 2001 he released *"Love and Theft"*—it rose to number 5. *Modern Times* at number one in 2006 was momentum—a steady, slowly unfolding campaign against Fitzgerald's pronouncement—against himself, really—that there are no second acts in American lives. Throughout this time, from 1997 to 2006, Bob Dylan played more than a thousand shows, from the Sun Palace in Fukuoka, Japan, to the 9:30 Club in Washington, D.C., in forty-seven states and twenty-six countries. In the presidential campaign year of 2000, he visited thirty-two states, which may have been more than either Al Gore or George W. Bush did. From "Crash on the Levee" at Hall "A" in Tokyo on February 9, 1997, to "The Levee's Gonna Break" at New York City Center on November 20, 2006, he played hundreds of different songs.

Time Out of Mind, "Love and Theft," and *Modern Times* raised Bob Dylan to a plateau of heroic irrelevancy he has not left since. He can put out unique and mysterious albums, as with *Tempest* in 2012 ("The streets have names that you can't pronounce," he sang in "Scarlet Town," a song about what it would mean to grow up in the town where Barbara Allen died), that are hardly noticed. He can issue an album of Christmas songs and two collections of so-called Sinatra songs that provoke amusement at best, and then a three-album set of thirty more such songs, from "Once Upon a Time" to "How Deep the Ocean" to "But Beautiful" to "When the World Was Young," that so knit together the moods of the American Century—the official, *Life* magazine version of the pre- and postwar periods—that it rewrote that time, bringing it into the present like a folk memory, as if any songs so taken to heart by so many people were folk songs by default, and elicit barely any recognition at all. He can put out a seventeen-minute song about the assassination of President Kennedy and a disc jockey, and get the whole world talking.

Each of those three albums that set this cycle in motion ended with a long song about someone facing his own oblivion: with a washed-up, alcoholic Philip Marlowe's jaded eye, as with "Highlands" on *Time Out of Mind,* with curses burrowing into a golden melody with "Sugar Baby" on *"Love and Theft."* With "Ain't Talkin'," as you listen, that one song can seem like a reflecting back of Bob Dylan's whole career, as he called it up in something he said to Richard Avedon's collaborator Doon Arbus around the time "Highlands" was first being heard. "One of the feelings" of the old folk world, he said, "was that you were a part of a very elite, special group of people that was outside and downtrodden. You felt like you were part of a different community, a more secretive one . . . That's been destroyed. I don't know what destroyed it. Some people say it's still there. I hope it is . . . I hope it is. I know, in my mind, that I'm still a member of a secret community. I might be the only one, you know?" And it can sometimes seem as if "Ain't Talkin'," as with *Time Out of Mind, "Love and Theft,"* and *Modern Times,* if you think of them as a single work, describes as much as anything else a quest to find a place for someone walking with a toothache in his heel, which is what Bob Dylan has been doing since he sang the first sodden line of *Time Out of Mind,* which brought Fats Domino into the story along with all the rest: "I'm walking—"

THE TIMES THEY ARE A-CHANGIN'

1964

"I sang a lot of 'come all you' songs," Bob Dylan said in 2015 in his MusiCares address, telling the tale of his whole musical life. "There's plenty of them. There's way too many to be counted. 'Come along boys and listen to my tale / Tell you of my troubles on the old Chisholm Trail.' Or, 'Come all ye good people, listen while I tell / The fate of Floyd Collins, a lad we all know well.' "

"Come all ye fair and tender ladies / Take warning how you court your men / They're like a star on a summer morning / They first appear and then they're gone again." And then there's this one, "Gather 'round, people / A story I will tell / 'Bout Pretty Boy Floyd, the outlaw / Oklahoma knew him well."

If you sung all these "come all ye" songs all the time like I did, you'd be writing, "Come gather 'round people where ever you roam, admit that the waters around you

157

have grown / Accept that soon you'll be drenched to the bone / If your time to you is worth saving / And you better start swimming or you'll sink like a stone / The times they are a-changin'."

You'd have written that too. There's nothing secret about it. You just do it subliminally and unconsciously, because that's all enough, and that's all you know. That was all that was dear to me.

"Come senators, congressmen, please heed the call / Don't stand in the doorway, don't block up the hall / For he who gets hurt will be he who has stalled / The battle outside ragin' / Will soon shake your windows and rattle your walls / For the times they are a-changin'"—as with "Blowin' in the Wind" the year before, in 1964 it seemed obvious. Obvious who was who, what was up and what was down, who was trying to make history and who was trying to stop it. The song was so programmatic it could have been written by a committee. The come-all-ye tradition tipped right over into the finger-pointing tradition, the right side calling out the wrong side in a big, righteous march to shout down the walls of Jericho. "The pep rally, the Sousa march, the football cheer"—it could have been written as an illustration for *Little Sandy Review*'s "P-FOR-PROTEST." "It was ironic that Bob Dylan's picture should have been placed next to Jerry Lewis's on the recent ESQUIRE cover awarding the dubious achievements for 1964," Paul Nelson and Jon Pankake wrote in the last number of *Little Sandy Review,* in early 1965.

Those sad, sensitive eyes are a kind of counterpart of Lewis's grimace. Both of them have serious strivings beyond their actual abilities; both are victims of the show biz syndrome; both are clownish entertainers to a popular audience incapable of understanding anything but their very broadest effects; both are idolized by a cult of pseudo-intellectuals who rationalize their shortcomings and attempt to read profundity into every whim, the symbol of the universe in every cast-off cigarette butt; both began with promising early work and grew into Great Men, One-Man Shows, etc., with black-and-blue ribs from the nudgings of the VARIETY-BILLBOARD hustlers. We think Dylan and Lewis will pass from popularity very unhappy and dissatisfied artists, wondering where it all went wrong. Lewis will go back to screenings of Chaplin and Dylan to recordings of Woody, attempting to fathom the ingenious, complex simplicity that at one time seemed so accessible to them both. The problem of our times, in one way: The fans scream and mob me, folks, but deep down inside, I know I really haven't got it. They're detestable—or am I? Where are the love and promises I wanted to share with them? Why did art die when I'm alive and willing to sacrifice my life to produce it?

"I used to care, but things have changed," you could have heard Bob Dylan sing in Curtis Hanson's film *Wonder Boys* in 2000. He started with lines from "Worried Man Blues"; the lead instrument was a stick on a snare drum, keeping an unchanging beat. The tone of the singing was so full of distance, irony, and amusement over the singer's own hobbled stance in particular and the foibles of mankind in general that "Don't get up gentlemen, I'm only passing through" felt far more alive, more dramatic, than "All the truth in the world adds up to one big lie." "I used to care"—it wasn't a personal statement, Bob Dylan telling the world where he himself stood now, but something far more political: more a matter of one person seeing himself in others. Regardless of where any song begins, whether in private sentiment or public catastrophe, if it achieves any shape at all it ceases to be what the person putatively in charge thought it was when he or she first turned on the light. It becomes a fiction: here, someone trying on the role of someone who didn't care, to see where it would take him, what words it would turn up, what rhythm the story needed for it to come across, what it would tell him about a world where, as a presidential election played out, maybe no one did care. It could leave the listener wondering if the whole thing wasn't one big joke, a feint, someone slipping the left hook history throws at anyone almost sixty who still thinks he has something to prove.

"Things Have Changed" won an Oscar, which over the next year Dylan displayed on stage on top of an amplifier. The more you listened, the more the question turned around: things have changed. Do you care? Did you ever? If Mr. Voice of a Generation, Mr. Jesus Is Coming, Mr. Wiggle Wiggle said he didn't care, was there any reason not to believe him? Was there any reason to care whether he ever cared or not? Who cares what Bob Dylan thinks? But the smile under the words as he sang them never dimmed. Whoever was singing this song was having a very good time. The times they are a-changin'? Things *have* changed. That's how history is made, or dissolved, when you step back and say, nothing ever really happened, and nothing ever will. Everything about "The Times They Are A-Changin'" felt obvious; nothing in "Things Have Changed" did. The whole song turned on the line most easy to miss, buried in the middle of a verse: "Just for a second I thought I saw something move." Just for a second I thought I felt history take a step, which means that history is real, that I am part of it, that I can't escape it, that I don't want to. But it was a trick of the light. The song kept up its quietly relentless pace, standing still in 4/4 time.

On January 6, 2021, "The Times They Are A-Changin'" didn't seem obvious, and history exposed how vulnerable it really was. The people flooding through the Capitol, smearing feces on the marble, hoisting Confederate flags as John Calhoun and Charles Sumner looked down from the walls, smashing into the Senate chamber, beating police to the ground and kicking them where they lay, weren't chanting, "Come senators, congressmen, please heed the call / Don't stand in the doorways, don't block up the hall," but they could have been. Instead they sang "Old Dan Tucker," shouting *Get out of the way you fucking n----- at black Capitol policemen—"They're saying: 'Trump is our rightful president. Nobody voted for Biden,'"* Capitol officer Harry Dunn said later. "I needed to catch my breath. So I said: 'I voted for Joe Biden. What? My vote doesn't count?' A woman responded, 'This n----- voted for Joe Biden!' Everybody that was there started joining in. 'Hey, n-----!' It was over 20 people who said it."

Two months later I walked into NC, a now-shuttered coffee shop on Washington Avenue in Minneapolis. On the wall over the turntable behind the counter—what you saw when you ordered—was a display of LP jackets: Billy Joel's *The Stranger,* Willie Nelson's *For the Good Times,* Joni Mitchell's *For the Roses,* Elton John's *Greatest Hits,* and *The Times They Are A-Changin'.* All but the last looked dull, like cheap advertising, with whatever aura, of art, or of success, they might have carried long corroded. The squinting face and stark posture of the person on the Dylan album still communicated an undimmed questioning. It held its moment. But even more than that, it made its own moment, tossed its past into the present, and retained the power to put you on the spot. There were many better songs on the album than the title song—"Ballad of Hollis Brown," "With God on Our Side," "North Country Blues," "Boots of Spanish Leather," "Restless Farewell," "The Lonesome Death of Hattie Carroll" most of all—but was the old warhorse, the old protest song, the old catchphrase, the old cliché, merely a relic, "giving form to passing fashions, epitomizing a certain style," another cigarette butt from "a once-brilliant manipulator of cultural signs"? Not, somehow, on that wall, fifty-seven years later; fifty-seven years later it carried "Things Have Changed" along with it. "In the mid-Sixties," Paul Nelson wrote ten years after that final, 1965 editorial in *Little Sandy Review*, "Dylan's talent evoked such an intense degree of personal participation from both his admirers and detractors that he could not be permitted so much as a random action. Hungry for a sign, the world used to follow him around, just waiting for him to drop a cigarette butt. When he did they'd sift through the remains, looking for significance. The scary part is they'd find it—and it really would be significant."

So this is a book of cigarette butts. Like the sign that, not long after the album cover display went up in NC, just as the murder trial of Derek Chauvin for the death of George Floyd the year before was about to begin in Minneapolis, began to appear here and there in the Uptown district of the city, a neighborhood of small shops and a few restaurants and coffeehouses and bars, slightly bohemian around the edges: a sign unfolding as part of a mural on the siding of a shut-down movie theater, or in a recessed wall on a residential street behind a hardware store. There it was big, maybe six feet wide and eight feet tall. The top half was made of broad, vertical, blurred rectangles, the half-images piled on top of each other, looking like a field of raised arms. Creeping up from the bottom, fading out halfway, in red worked into the brown, were dozens of carefully drawn symbols, most in their own boxes, like the tiny hieroglyphs in a Chuck Close painting: triangles, empty squares, diagonal scores, crescents. The longer you looked, some tended toward abstractions of specific things: the American flag, a mug shot, a megaphone. And in the upper middle, on each side of a divide made by a raised concrete strip on the building, with florid white, commercial stenciling inside two deep circles, someone was playing that NC album again, the odd capitalizations signaling that the artist was the author of the words as much as anyone: "DON'T Criticize WHAT you can't UNDER-STAND" on the left, "for the times THEY ARE a-CHANGING" on the right. Or like the painting the Los Angeles artist Henry Taylor made in 2017, on the shooting death the year before of Philando Castile, in the St. Paul suburb of Falcon Heights, just miles from where the Uptown murals went up five years later. Castile was driving with his girlfriend, Diamond Reynolds, in the front and her four-year-old daughter, Dae'Anna, in the back. He was stopped by officer Jeronimo Yanez because, Yanez said later, Castile looked like a robbery suspect because of his broad nose, though he told Castile it was a matter of a broken taillight. Castile informed Yanez that he was carrying a legally permitted handgun. Yanez shot him five times as Reynolds used Facebook to live-stream Castile's body slumped in his seat. For a work that hung in the 2017 Whitney Biennial along with Dana Schutz's shattering *Open Casket,* picturing Emmett Till as in 1955 in Chicago his mother, Mamie Till, exposed to the world the torture and death inflicted on him in Mississippi, Henry Taylor began with frames from Diamond Reynolds's shaking video footage. The image he made, too, was slightly off-kilter. It showed a white hand pointing a gun through a car window as a black man lay dead in his seat, without the huge red spread of blood on his stomach in Reynolds's film, without her in the seat next to him, without her daughter, a man alone with his left eye open and fixed. The painting was the same size as the stencil in Minneapolis, six by eight feet, a virtual mural of its own. The picture exploded with color: the police officer's black uniform, his white arm, the car's green interior, Castile's blue seatbelt, white T-shirt, brown skin, the dark ceiling of the car, the yellow-orange of the street filling the car windows, what might be a glimpse of blue sky and a white cloud. It was overwhelmingly still. It was imagined; it was a fact. Jeronimo Yanez was charged with murder and acquitted. The painting carried the title THE TIMES THAY AINT A CHANGING, FAST ENOUGH!

DESOLATION ROW

1965

In 1959, in a Nashville recording session for Marty Rob-bins's song "El Paso," the guitarist Grady Martin played a twisting, romantic, ten-second south-of-the-border figure to open the song. Robbins came in with his deep, reflec-tive first words, the first line of the song that would seal the singer's death warrant: "Out in the West Texas town of El Paso—" With that acoustic guitar leading through-out, the song, produced by Don Law, who in 1936 and 1937 had produced Robert Johnson,* was a number one hit and, at over four and a half minutes, before Bob Dylan's six-minute "Like a Rolling Stone" perhaps the longest Top 10 recording on a single side of a 45.

---

* "At the time," John Hammond once said of producing *The Free-wheelin' Bob Dylan*, "I was saying, 'Bobby, you should be recording in Nash-ville.' . . . one night we were recording 'Oxford Town,'" a song about the murderous white riot that greeted James Meredith's enrollment in 1962 as the first African-American student at the University of Mississippi. "And Don Law, who was the head of our Nashville operation, was in the building, and I said, 'Don, you have got to come up and hear this kid. Because he's a genius and he's got to work with Nashville musicians. We don't have the

Six years later, in New York, at a session following that for "Like a Rolling Stone," for "Desolation Row" the producer Bob Johnston brought in the Nashville guitarist Charlie McCoy, who with Dylan's light but insistent strumming behind him began with eight strong, thick acoustic seconds that called up Robbins's song, rooting the twelve-minute tale Dylan was about to tell in the collective Top 40 memory of a cowboy ballad about murder and love that almost anyone who could have been expected to hear Dylan's own song would harbor. Dylan sang slowly, without affect, as if remembering something: "They're selling postcards of the hanging / They're painting the passports brown / The beauty parlor is full of sailors / The circus is in town." At least historically, the lines had a precursor—which Dylan could have found in John Lomax's 1919 *Songs of the Cattle Trail and Cow Camp:* "The Clown's Baby," a verse by one Margaret Vandergrift, author of the 1889 collection *The Dead Doll and Other Poems.* "It was on the western frontier / The miners, rugged and brown / Were gathered round the posters / The circus had come to

---

kind of guys around here who can play for him.' . . . Don Law came in and listened to the lyrics of 'Oxford Town,' and said, 'My god, John. He could never do this kind of thing in Nashville. You're crazy.' And walked out of the studio." Hammond had already given Dylan a prerelease copy of Robert Johnson's *King of the Delta Blues Singers*, the first official issue of Johnson's songs since the 1930s, which had shocked him to the core: "I immediately differentiated between him and anyone else I had ever heard," he wrote in *Chronicles*. "Johnson masked the presence of twenty men." What wouldn't Bob Dylan have given to make records with the man who made records with Robert Johnson?

town!" But Bob Dylan was singing about a different kind of circus. "Even if Desolation Row is not his greatest song (I might make the case for 4–5 others, depending on the year)," Joshua Clover wrote in 2021, "it's where all the bodies are buried."

When "Desolation Row" appeared in 1965, as the last song on *Highway 61 Revisited*—a song about an invisible bohemia surrounded by a Puritan republic of mystification and repression—few people knew that in the first decades of the twentieth century, there had been a craze for postcards of lynchings of black Americans by crowds of white Americans, events that then took place seemingly by the day—postcards sent through the U.S. mail, traded among collectors, sold in souvenir shops and at county fairs. And even fewer knew that a postcard depicting the lynching of three black circus workers, Elias Clayton, Elmer Jackson, and Isaac McGhie, in Duluth, in 1920, twenty-one years before Bob Dylan was born there—Irene Tusken, a white woman, accused four men of rape, and while there was no evidence, and while she said she had passed out as soon as the attack began and never saw the faces of the men, could recognize them "only by their size and physique"—was among the most popular of all. And there is no telling whether Bob Dylan's grandfather, Zigman Zimmerman, born in Odessa, in Ukraine, in 1876, and in 1920 a thriving Prudential insurance salesman, or Dylan's father, Abram, or Abe, Zimmerman, who was born in Duluth and would have been eight at the time, were in the crowd.

Bob Dylan may not know, and probably would not say either way. It was not the sort of thing that was talked about—even if one can imagine Abe Zimmerman, who, Bob Dylan would write in 2004, "wasn't so sure that the truth would set anybody free," taking his son aside one evening, maybe after his bar mitzvah, opening the door to a closet filled with old family albums and legal documents, the kind of place kids would never get into, taking out a yellowed postcard: *This is something you ought to know about.*

Is there any right to think that way, to even in the most spectral and speculative way mark people who cannot speak for themselves with complicity? I don't know. But the Duluth lynching was a cataclysmic event in Minnesota. In horror or exultation it implicated everyone. The governor was the president of the St. Paul NAACP. Newspapers proclaimed the lynchings a stain on the state. It was not out of the news. A fourth accused rapist, Max Mason, was caught in the town of Virginia, just over from Hibbing, convicted and sentenced to thirty years in prison—and then released in 1925, on the bizarre condition that he leave the state and not return until 1941. He died in 1942. On June 12, 2020, eighteen days after George Floyd was murdered in Minneapolis, Mason was granted the first posthumous pardon in Minnesota history, announced by Governor Tim Walz, on the grounds that no rape had taken place: "This is one hundred years overdue." Three dozen men were arrested for mob action. The legislature passed an antilynching law—"Yet, by 1992," the historian

William D. Green said of his arrival in Minnesota from the South, and perhaps could have said in 1922, "it was as if the event had never occurred. I had never heard of it. No one I knew had heard of it." There are no more references to the Duluth lynchings in "Desolation Row," and the song is not about them anymore than it is about Albert Einstein, Bette Davis, or the *Titanic,* all of which appear in it. But the connection of a specific, publicly historical event, even if hidden, or especially if hidden, and a possibly private version of a historical event, and their connection in turn to the idea of a haven of free speech and free identity called Desolation Row, a place not on any map, that can only be spoken of in metaphors and riddles, but at the same time is the only place where one can feel truly oneself and truly acknowledge others, may not be an illusion. And to follow that possible connection, drawing on knowledge of how people move through history, how they disappear from it as history is erased, and how, sometimes in history books, sometimes in movies or paintings or songs, history is reclaimed, restaged, and rewritten, you may have to speculate.

It is certain that neither Abe Zimmerman, or Bob Dylan, learned about the Duluth lynching in the Duluth or Hibbing public schools they attended, any more than the Tulsa Massacre of 1921—where as many as three hundred black citizens were murdered, shot, burned, and hanged from lampposts as a white mob destroyed the Greenwood district, the most prosperous black community in the country, celebrated as Black Wall Street—was taught in school in Tulsa. As with other public lynchings, particularly outside the South, silence smothered the event almost immediately. Those who committed lynchings were rarely charged, and after initial reports their names were never printed in any newspaper or publicly discussed. As William Green says, within a few years it would be as if the event never happened. But it would survive as a rumor, a story whispered by adults out of earshot of their children, who would pick up fragments of a tale they could not complete, but which perhaps made them curious, even to the point of asking their parents what they were talking about, a curiosity that might remain when they were told, "Nothing."

In San Jose, California, in 1933, two local drifters, inspired by the Lindbergh kidnapping of the year before, kidnapped Brooke Hart, the son of the richest man in town—someone, as it happened, who was the pride of the city, a Jewish golden boy who condescended to no one and who was liked, if not idolized, by nearly everyone who knew him.

The two men immediately killed Brooke Hart—they tied him up, smashed his skull, weighted him with concrete, threw him off the low-hanging San Mateo Bridge, and shot him in the water. They were arrested almost as soon as they made their ransom demands. They were broken out of the San Jose jail with a battering ram by a crowd of citizens, taken to the park across the street, stripped naked, sexually mutilated, and hanged from a single tree.

Everyone knew the lynching was going to happen. People came from as far away as Los Angeles to be there. Earl Warren, the district attorney of Alameda County, which then included San Jose, announced that anyone taking part would be prosecuted and punished. In response the governor, Sunny Jim Rolph, issued a blanket pardon in advance.

Even though in a speech in Nuremberg that year Adolf Hitler seized on the event as proof of the degeneracy of democracy, with crowds rallying for a Jew, as with Duluth this event was taken out of history and banished from public discourse. Even though there were at least two very fictionalized films based on the lynchings (Fritz Lang's celebrated *Fury* in 1936 for MGM, and the 1950 Lloyd Bridges–Frank Lovejoy B-picture *The Sound of Fury*—changed to *Try and Get Me* after MGM threatened to sue), there were never any Where-Are-They-Now features on the twenty-fifth or fiftieth anniversaries of the event in the San Jose or San Francisco papers ("Today Earl Warren is the Chief Justice of the United States Supreme Court"), let alone on radio or television. As in Duluth, it was, purposefully and effectively, as if it had never happened. There were distant stories, some sense that something bad had taken place, once, but for children, nowhere to look.

In 1992 the first book on the San Jose lynchings was published, and my parents went to hear the author at Kepler's Books in Menlo Park—at its original location, a few blocks away, in the sixties one of the sole Peninsula outposts of bohemia, along with the foreign film theater up the street and a coffeehouse called St. Michael's Alley in

Palo Alto. The then-old-timey jug band guitarist Jerry Garcia was always at Kepler's. Ira Sandperl, my eighth-grade creative writing teacher and later founder of Joan Baez's Institute for the Study of Nonviolence, worked the counter. The new place was spiffy and modern. A man came in and sat down next to my parents, noticed their age, and asked them if they remembered the lynching. Yes, they said—and that my father was born and grew up in San Jose and was sixteen in 1933; my mother was from San Francisco and was ten. The man asked my father if he had known Brooke Hart; he said yes. He asked if they knew anyone who had been at the lynching; they said yes. The man turned to my father and said, *Were you there?* He told me, later, that people had asked him if he wanted to go, but he told them he had homework to do and he couldn't.

My father finished his story. "Would you like to know who asked him to go?" my mother said. I thought it must have been a bunch of his high-school friends, whoever they might have been—I'd never met any. "Your grandparents," she said.

A lynching was entertainment, spectacle, even sport. It was also, like the Irish and then Jews putting on blackface until, in the words of the historian Michael Rogin, they could be "washed white," a ritual of Americanism, an exercise in civic loyalty, civic justice, and community solidarity. It wasn't something a respectable businessman like my grandfather, or my grandmother, his business partner, could afford to boycott—even if it was a proud family legend that my grandfather was the only member of the

San Jose Chamber of Commerce to vote against buying machine guns to keep the refugees from the Dust Bowl, the Okies, out of town. If you didn't attend, you would have to explain why. So my grandparents, whatever they thought of what they knew was going to happen, had to be there.

The same might be true for Bob Dylan's grandfather—and it isn't impossible that Zigman Zimmerman brought his son with him that night to be part of the town's history, and that, under a cloud of don't ask, don't tell, hidden public history might have become hidden family history. And given that Bob Dylan is an imaginative artist, even if he didn't know if his grandfather or his father had been present at the lynching when he recorded "Desolation Row" forty-five years later, or even if he knew they were not, he could have imagined that they were—which is to say, in an artist's sense, that he was.

JIM JONES

1992

In the most striking scene in *Chronicles,* Bob Dylan walks the reader into a classic grand Greenwich Village party, hosted by a classic Greenwich Village grande dame— it could be Mabel Dodge, in her salon with the likes of Emma Goldman, John Reed, Margaret Sanger, and Big Bill Haywood at her Fifth Avenue apartment near Washington Square Park, but here it's the folk music patron Camilla Adams. It's sometime in early April 1961, and as Dylan and Delores Dixon come through the doors of the top-floor apartment of what he calls a Romanesque mansion, "on 5th Avenue, near Washington Square Park," it's a set piece, just as Camilla Adams could as likely be a literary device as a real-life folk-world Peggy Guggenheim "who looked like Ava Gardner." It could be a hundred parties, or rumors, you-should-have-been-theres, but it's irresistible—and for all the philistine Dylan biographers who have dismissed their subject's own book as a farrago of invention, of people who didn't exist and incidents that could have never happened (leaving aside the resentment of those who can't bear the possibility that Bob Dylan might know something about his life that they don't), it escapes them that Dylan's pages on the allure of folk music in the early 1960s are for spirit and emotion the most accurate there are. So for this place and time, as Walter Cronkite would have said if he'd been covering the party, you are there.

The event is a "bon voyage" for Cisco Houston—the Clark Gable of folk music, road buddy of Woody Guthrie and Burl Ives ("played together at migrant camps during the Great Depression"), at heart more an actor than a singer ("People said he could have been a movie star," Dylan writes, as if writing in his notebook, not in a real book more than forty years later, "that he once turned down a role opposite Myrna Loy"), with a well-modulated, TV host's voice, every word distinct, even polite—who would be dead of cancer at forty-two before the month was out. "I could see the rooms were already swarming with people, the bohemian crowd—a lot of old-timers," Dylan says. "The air was thick with perfume and cigarette smoke and the smell of whiskey and a lot of people"—you can hear Dylan's "Million Dollar Bash" playing under the pages. You can hear Randy Newman's "Mama Told Me Not to Come." "The apartment was very Victorian, deco-rated with a lot of lovely things. Beaux Arts lamps, carved boudoir chairs, couches in plush velvet—heavy andirons connected with chains by the fireplace and the fireplace was blazing." There's Pete Seeger, with his manager Harold Leventhal, once Guthrie's, a power. There's a man who had once been Mae West's boyfriend, a shadow of a New York legend, like the woman in the Guthrie Village-party jape "Walt Whitman's Niece." There's the downtown filmmaker Ken Jacobs, Theodore Bikel, and Moe Asch, head of Folkways Records. There's the cowboy artist Harry Jackson, who "looked like General Grant." Soon enough he'd have Dylan sit for an already clichéd portrait: newsboy cap, guitar in lap, head slightly back, eyes closed over the suffering in his song, cigarette in his mouth.

There's Houston and his labor friends, who looked like "tugboat captains or baggy-pantsed outfielders," Communist organizers kicked out when the CIO merged with the AFL, including Mack McKenzie, there with Eve McKenzie, once a Martha Graham dancer, one of the couples who put Dylan up over many nights. There's the performance artist before the name Robyn Whitlaw, who liked to break the law and call it art and get away with it, and Irwin Silber, the editor of *Sing Out!,* a keeper of the flame, who wanted folk music to take over the world without going commercial. Among many actors, Broadway, Off-Broadway, there's Diana Sands from *A Raisin in the Sun.* There's Lee Hayes of the Weavers, who had a number one hit for thirteen weeks in 1950 with a cleaned-up version of Lead Belly's "Goodnight, Irene" before being blacklisted—he went back to the early forties with Houston, and with Seeger and Guthrie in the Almanac Singers, performing labor songs and antiwar songs, anti-Roosevelt, anti-Churchill, at least until Hitler invaded the Soviet Union and the line changed. There's Erik Darling of the Rooftop Singers, who in 1963 would take a version of "Walk Right In," a 1929 tune by the Memphis band Cannon's Jug Stompers, the kind of folk musicians the folklorist and performer John Cohen of the New Lost City Ramblers would call "mystical gods," to the top of the charts. There are the folk revival icons Sonny Terry and Brownie McGhee, from Georgia and Tennessee.

There's Harry Belafonte, "the best balladeer in the land," "learned songs directly from Leadbelly and Woody Guthrie," who over two pages Dylan sets forth as a colossus, a man he'd never be, writing as if everything, present and future, was running through his mind as he looked into the room in Camilla Adams's place to peer at Belafonte without embarrassing himself, poking back at the Belafonte satires he'd read in *Little Sandy Review:* "The folk purists had a problem with him, but Harry—who could have kicked the shit out of all of them, couldn't be bothered, said that all folksingers were interpreters, said it in a public way as if someone had summoned him to set the record straight . . . Astoundingly and as unbelievable as it might have seemed, I'd be making my professional recording debut with Harry, playing harmonica on one of his albums called *Midnight Special.* Strangely enough, this was the only one memorable recording date that would stand out in my mind for years to come. Even my own sessions would become lost in abstractions. With Belafonte I felt like I'd been anointed in some kind of way." But this night, even more than Belafonte, there was Mike Seeger.

He was from the Seeger family, son of the composer Charles Seeger, a musicologist who taught at Harvard and Berkeley, a founding member of the Communist Party cell the Composers Collective. Taking the Party name Carl Sands, he believed the music that would rouse the masses to revolution was in Hans Eisler's twelve-tones, until Thomas Hart Benton, when they were both teaching at the New School for Social Research in Greenwich Village, converted him to the 1927 Brunswick recordings of the Virginia mountain singer and banjo player Dock Boggs. Seeger heard Boggs's demonic "Pretty Polly," the wasted life of his "Country Blues," a sound that prised from traditional songs a sense of indomitability, a face of defiance, that raised the voice of the folk to a heroic plane. A different road to the new world opened up. "Little Maggie" and "Buddy Won't You Roll Down the Line," to say nothing of "John Henry," could be recast as calls to the struggle. Songs about the yearning for lost love or even lovers' murders could be transposed into songs about the yearning of the working class and its ability to rise up and make its own history—songs to which the people would respond instinctively. The music would play the chords of common memory—or, as the historian William Hogeland puts it more bluntly, to Charles Seeger "folk music existed outside the corruption and alienation of bourgeois culture; it needed only integration with Party ideology to become a means of worker empowerment."

From that point on the Seeger household was a folk house: the composer Ruth Crawford Seeger, Charles Seeger's second wife, began transcribing scores for folk songs recorded in the first decades of the century by John Lomax and Alan Lomax, creating the founding collections of American vernacular music for the Library of Congress. Elizabeth Cotton, the family housekeeper and a distinctive singer, guitarist, and composer herself, would become a folk icon in the 1950s and sixties with her song "Freight Train."* Three of Seeger's seven children became folk singers. Pete (1919–2014), from Charles Seeger's first marriage to the violinist Constance de Clyver Edson, and Peggy, born in 1935, followed their father's politics. Pete started out in the thirties, adopting a southern accent and the more working-class Party name Pete Bowers while put-

---

* Though an awful report in *Little Sandy Review* no. 12 on the First Annual University of Chicago Folk Festival exposes what, with the almost exclusively white, middle-class makeup of the modern folk audience, that might have been worth: "Leading the relatively sheltered lives we do in Minneapolis, we poor country boys were startled by our first contact with big city 'folk cult' members. Shaggy persons were crawling out of the woodwork singing and playing THE SLOOP JOHN B, BANUA, LONESOME TRAVELER, and other old-time favorites. Every guitar strumming girl seemed to be ecstatically belting out VIRGIN MARY in tones as close to Joan Baez's as she could muster. Off in a corner, some of the higher-echelon pickers were dazzling wide-eyed boys and girls with their fantastic, vacant-eyed guitar picking—composed of equal parts blues and bluegrass, and played at a dizzying gait. No art or style, but plenty of razzle-dazzle . . . Some of these kids could technically have played rings around many of the original performers, but whatever they were playing (we couldn't figure it out), it wasn't folk music. Libba Cotton took out her guitar and began warming up for the evening concert, and immediately a girl with long, stringy hair and black stockings was worshipping at her feet (literally). One could picture her a few years back doing much the same thing for Elvis. Mrs. Cotton played and sang I DON'T LOVE NOBODY in her intimate, gracious way; whereupon the girl shrilled, 'That's on your album. We've heard it before. Why don't you do something NEW?' She finally snatched the guitar out of Libba's hands and began whining, 'How do you do it? Show me how to do it, huh? Show me how to do it.'"

ting his prep school and Harvard past behind him; Peggy made her name in England in the fifties and sixties with her husband, Ewan MacColl, a songwriter and singer who as a force in the cultural section of the British Communist Party was also the commissar of the British folk world, dictating through a network of folk clubs what songs could be sung and how. Mike Seeger was born in 1933; he died in 2009 at seventy-five, with another lifetime's work to do. He followed the crumbs dropped by Dock Boggs, who had disappeared from history after his last recording session in 1929. In 1963 Mike found him in the mining town of Norton, Virginia, where he'd always been, and Boggs, who died in 1971 on his seventy-third birthday, a retired mine worker living on Social Security and his UMW pension, took up his banjo, which he'd gotten out of hock only months before, as if sensing that after more than thirty years it was time again to play it, and sang. He sang first in his living room, then at the Newport Folk Festival, then all around the country.

But by that time Mike Seeger had for years been seeking what, in that line from the Gospel of John his father might not have appreciated, he called the true vine. "I am the true vine," as Jesus says: "now ye are clean through the word which I have spoken to you." To Mike Seeger that cleansing meant the old American music found on 78s from the twenties and thirties, now in the mid-fifties spirited out of libraries, taped overnight, then secreted back on their shelves. It meant the living avatars who sang on those same records, Clarence Ashley, Mississippi John

Hurt, Buell Kazee, Bascom Lamar Lunsford, Furry Lewis, Skip James, and more, some of them playing at fiddlers' conventions in the South, some of them tracked down by record collectors like Stanley looking for Livingston, some of them brought to Alan Lomax's folk-song soirées in his downtown walk-up apartment: "Well, you're in Greenwich Village now," he says to someone's film camera sometime in the early sixties, all but licking his lips after ushering eager young people through his door like a heavy-lidded Pied Piper, Sonny Terry's harmonica playing in the background, "where people come to get away from America." To Mike Seeger, Ashley and the rest were where you went to discover America. As a living musician that meant spinning an inheritance to which he had staked his own claim into the way the songs came to second, third, ninth lives under his own fingers. In 1958, with John Cohen and Tom Paley, he'd formed the New Lost City Ramblers. Across hundreds of tunes embodying the musical heritage of the country song by song, in the flesh, they tried to live out the music as they played it. Sometimes, not always, they could feel it happen—as it happened in 2009, the year Mike Seeger died, for a New School student named Maddie Deutch. For a class on Lee Smith's novel *The Devil's Dream,* she was standing in front of her classmates on a late afternoon in early December to sing an untitled song Smith made up to describe the first manifestation of the curse of folk music down seven generations of a Virginia mountain family.

It's in the 1830s. Moses Bailey marries Kate Malone. Moses is a seeker after God, but Kate loves the fiddle: "the voice," Moses says, "of the devil laughing." He forbids her to play it, and his children too. Moses is insane, but not so that anyone would stop him: in the mountains, no one expects anyone to be like everybody else. One day Moses leaves home to earn money; he'll be gone a week, he says. But he's traveling by river, his raft crashes, and he walks home. He hears Kate and his children singing and playing, and he falls on them like a fire, beating his wife and his sons, Jeremiah and Ezekiel, and his daughter, Mary. The children escape into the woods. Jeremiah dies that day. Moses dies soon after. Kate goes mad. The ballad of Kate Malone is heard in the mountains not long after. Smith prints only the words she wrote, but if you read them out loud, playing beneath them you can hear the melody of "The Cuckoo," a song that will work its way through the whole of the story Smith tells. "And so as I walked up to the front of the room," Deutch wrote later, "the last ounce of daylight seeping in through the big rippled windows, I felt the classroom melt around me. The walls became an expanse of forest, with huge pines popping up in corners of the room. The dry wood floors beneath my feet turned to soft earth that gathered up under my heels. I could see fireflies darting in and out of the fold up chairs which had become tree stumps, overgrown mushrooms, and beds of wildflowers." Facing audiences in fold-up chairs in rooms the same size, in the same Greenwich Village neighbor-hood near Washington Square Park, there were nights when the New Lost City Ramblers played "The Cuckoo" and felt just like that—and so did the people listening.

Onstage they dressed like accountants from the 1920s, in vests, stiff white shirts, dark ties, even metal sleeve bands. They clowned, they made fun of their own scholasticism, but their dedication to the music of the past, the folk music that even in the twenties was sold as "old-time," was absolute. With Cohen's warm smile and Paley's plain face, Seeger drew the eye: his sharp, angular features let him look like a hanging judge when he chose to. To Robert Cantwell, writing in 1996, as "a face and figure on a light, elfin-like physical frame," Seeger was "essentially out of the past, the very image of the storied frontiersman whose music he has been all his life reinventing, a smaller edition, it might be said, of Abraham Lincoln." It was an affinity that might have occurred to Seeger himself, as with the Lincoln beard he sometimes wore, but however Seeger might appear—with his shadowed eyes, he could look as much like the 1956 Elvis Presley—the image spoke to the moral weight he communicated with his strongest songs. As Cantwell went on: "he creates a strange, swimming, otherworldly sound that might, to a willing listener, suggest the image of a sun-blinded western wagoner of the 1850s at the limits of his endurance, his understanding clouded, his heart hardened and hopeless, his spirit harrowed by some sublime delusion." And, with Dylan perhaps having read Cantwell as he himself wrote eight years after, in 2004, summoning the moment in that Fifth Avenue apartment, he does everything he can to go farther. "He was extraordinary," Dylan writes, before hitting his stride, "gave me an eerie feeling. Mike was unprecedented. He was like a duke, a knight errant. As for being a folk musician, he was the supreme archetype. He could push a stake through Dracula's black heart. He was the romantic, egalitarian and revolutionary type all at once—he had chivalry in his blood. Like some figure from a restored monarchy, he had come to purify the church."

You can hear that, as Bob Dylan would have heard it, in Mike Seeger's performance of "When First Unto This Country," as recorded with the New Lost City Ramblers at the first Newport Folk Festival in 1959. As an old American ballad it seems to carry with it the idea of America, but before Fitzgerald's Dutch sailors, before John Smith, before there were any new Americans to carry it out. It's the tale of a man who loves a woman who turns away, who won't be stayed, who steals a horse to reach her—though there is the faraway suggestion that he steals the horse because, though he's riding on his own horse to win his beloved, he wants this horse, "a fine gray, both plumb-looking and white," more, maybe even more than her. He is seized and beaten and with his hair cut off and his beard stripped thrown in jail to rot forever: "Till I wished to my own soul, that I'd never been a thief." He tells his story not because he's ready to tell it, but because he has nothing else to do with his life. On Seeger's path through the tale, you can hear it as it played out again and again, as each new immigrant tried to find their place in the country, to pursue the happiness, in whatever form it might take, they had heard was their new right.

Seeger learned the song from recordings of the Gant

Family Singers his parents had in the house—part of a set made by the Lomaxes in Austin, Texas, in 1934 and 1935.[*] Maggie and George Gant lived in a shack in Austin by the Colorado River; they had eight children. Family singing kept them going in the worst years of the Great Depression; they had a repertoire of over two hundred traditional songs, and the Lomaxes recorded more than forty. The one that still stands out today is "When First Unto This Country," as sung by Maggie Gant and her seventeen-year-old daughter Foy. Their voices are high, warbling in crossing lines, suppressing the melody, but extending certain words in each verse, as if the words are a step ahead of them and they have to catch up.

The music as Mike Seeger refashioned it is stately, measured, reflective, the song as it's designed asking anyone who sings it to consider each choice they make as they describe it. It's a feeling brought out when Seeger, following the Gants, but with a far more personal dramatization—though the words are the same, they are singing a song about someone else, and he is telling you

[*] Alan Lomax, then a student at the University of Texas, learned about the Gant family from his classmate John Henry Faulk, who was working on a degree in folklore. In the early 1950s, as a Will Rogers–style CBS radio host he was part of Alan's circle in New York. Named a Communist by a group calling itself Aware in 1956, he was blacklisted and banned from the air; in 1962 he won a huge libel suit against his accusers, and in the next year, in his return to the public eye, hosted *Folk Music and More Folk Music!*—a variety show that told the story of the United States from its founding to the present, through songs sung by Barbara Dane, the Staple Singers, the Brothers Four, Carolyn Hester, and Bob Dylan.

what happened to him—in a young, high, modest voice, a voice most of all unsure, wobbling between truth and lie, draws out the keynote word in each verse. *Courted, think, spied, carted, shaved, wished, coat*—but spied as *spyyyyyyed,* the word plumbed so deeply that the young man's voice, Seeger's voice, but also the voice of the man whose place he is taking, halts and almost breaks. *Courrrrrted, wissh-hhhhhed, coahhhhhht*—the words seem to leave the story that's being told and linger for a moment in a dream where every wish in the tale comes true. As a story, even cold on the page, it's desperate, heedless, so full of desire you can't believe the man who's telling you his tale will find the ending that he does any more than he can—but with the first line, "When first unto this country, a stranger I came," you see the whole story before it happens. As John Fahey wrote of "We met in the springtime," the first line of Hank Williams's "Alone and Forsaken": "By the fifth word you know it's all over."

That is coded in "When First Unto This Country." But when Mike Seeger stood to play it, he cast the spell of the song even before the first word was sung. He's less than fifteen seconds into the tune when, with John Cohen's banjo behind him, as Seeger strums his autoharp for the sweet, foreboding melody, lightly up and down, up and down, he pulls a high note out of the stiff strings. It can go straight to the heart and freeze it. It seems to hang in the air and then to burst, a burst of fate, even as notes follow it, smaller notes, but at the same pitch, pebbles rolling down a bank into a stream.

Right there, you've heard it all. You don't need to hear any more. You don't want to hear any more. Even if you've never heard a word of the song before, you already know too much. Put that note into that title and the story both begins and ends. Drive a stake through Dracula's dark heart: Mike Seeger could sing everything in a song without singing it.

He played everything, Dylan wrote, "whatever the song called for—the banjo, the fiddle, mandolin, autoharp, and the guitar, even harmonica in the rack . . . He was tense, poker-faced, and radiated telepathy . . . He played on all the various planes, the full index of the old-time styles, played in all the genres and had all the idioms mastered—Delta blues, ragtime, minstrel songs, buck-and-wing, dance reels, play party, hymns and gospel." It was overwhelming, enough to make a would-be so-called folk singer turn around and never come back: "It's not as if he just played everything well," Dylan wrote, "he played these songs as good as it was possible to play them." He stepped back, and took stock.

> I knew I was doing things right, was on the right road, was getting all the knowledge immediately and first-hand—memorizing words and melodies and changes, but now I saw that it could take me the rest of my life to make practical use of that knowledge and Mike didn't have to do that. He was just right there. He was too good and you can't be "too good," not in this world, anyway. In order to be as good as that, you'd just about

have to be him, and nobody else. Folk songs are eva-
sive—the truth about life, and life is more or less a
lie, but then again that's exactly the way we want it to
be . . . A folk song might vary in meaning and it might
not appear the same from one moment to the next. It
depends on who's playing and who's listening.

But now, in his moment, dwarfed by Seeger as a fact and
as an idea, an artist he would never be, he was only the
listener.

"The thought occurred to me," he set down in 2004,
summoning that night, "that I'd have to write my own folk
songs, ones that Mike didn't know."

And so he did: that is Bob Dylan's practical biography.
He rewrote the songbook and then the book took on a new
shape and all the credited sources that might have been
printed on the title page disappeared until only one was
left. He never forgot the old songs, but he gave them new
lives to live, and the old songs were so rich in melody and
paradox that like souls of the dead seeking new bodies they
could, in new hands, live forever. "Folk music is the only
music where it isn't simple," Dylan said in an interview in
1965, when he was accused of turning his back on it. "It's
weird . . . full of legend, myth, Bibles and ghosts . . . 'Little
Brown Dog.' 'I bought a little brown dog, its face is all grey.
Now I'm going to Turkey flying on my bottle.' And 'Nottamun Town,' that's like a herd of ghosts passing through on
the way to Tangiers." As he would say at the end of "Desolation Row," coming off the furious, pounding passage

from Charlie McCoy, who made his guitar sound like a whole orchestra, "I had to rearrange their faces / And give them all"—*ahhhhhlllll,* he sings, drawing out the word with satisfaction—"another name."

He wrote songs that as he put them out into the world wrapped their arms around history and then walked into it, songs that like gaudy cloaks of shadow and light wrapped themselves around the people who heard them and then brought them too into history, the history that was going on all around them and their own history as they pieced it together for themselves: "My mother and I drove into a small town, we were up in a little fishing cabin my grandpa built," the singer John Hiatt wrote in 2021. "She had to go to the drugstore, and she went in and 'Like a Rolling Stone' came on the radio. I was certain when she came back out, she wouldn't recognize me. I felt like the song had changed me that much, just by hearing it. I was 13 or so. I was transformed." That is The Bob Dylan Story: "Blowin' in the Wind." "I Shall Be Free," and "A Hard Rain's A-Gonna Fall." "Masters of War" and "With God on Our Side." *The Times They Are A-Changin'.* "It Ain't Me Babe" and "Motorpsycho Nitemare." "It's Alright, Ma (I'm Only Bleeding)" and "Mr. Tambourine Man." *Highway 61 Revisited* and *Blonde on Blonde.* "This Wheel's on Fire" and *John Wesley Harding.* "I Threw It All Away," "Sign on the Window," and "Knockin' on Heaven's Door." *Planet Waves* and *Blood on the Tracks.* "Isis." *Slow Train Coming* and from there through the desert of the 1980s, up toward the end of his fourth decade as a public artist. You could read in the papers whenever he appeared, from one city to another: a living legend.

But then, onstage in the late 1980s, into the early 1990s, he did an odd thing. At a certain point in some of his shows, most often alone, his band off the stage, he began to sing the old songs again, the songs Mike did know and was still performing, songs from those many New Lost City Ramblers albums, songs learned from other singers in Minneapolis and New York, from Harry Smith's anthology, Jon Pankake's 78s and Paul Nelson's LPs, on borrowed albums on obscure folk labels record stores didn't carry: material that in his repertoire predated that on his own first album. "Two Soldiers." "The Lakes of Pontchartrain." "Hills of the Buffalo." "Eileen Aroon." "The Waggoner's Lad." "Barbara Allen." "Wild Mountain Thyme." "The Golden Vanity." "Girl on the Green Briar Shore." "Little Moses." "When First Unto This Country." He sang them as if he'd been singing them all his life, and as if he was, still, like a private eye, trying to track them down. And it was strange: with song after song, at show after show, during these moments people in the crowd are giving out with drunken shouts, screaming, barking like dogs, hooting at the moon, whooping hippie whoops, as if to drown out this time-traveling relic who had suddenly appeared before them and if they keep it up will just as quickly disappear. "The audience slowed their chattering," Suze Rotolo wrote of hearing Dylan sing "Dink's Song" in a Philadelphia folk club in 1962. It was a traditional song, collected in Texas early in the twentieth century by John

Lomax, a song everybody did, even Llewyn Davis, of *course* Llewyn Davis, a song Dylan once claimed, maybe as a joke, maybe not, to have written: "He stilled the room. It was as though I had never heard the song before. He stilled my room, for sure." Against all the contempt such songs were bringing from his audience a quarter-century later, the singer seems at once defiant, some lone soldier defending the post after everyone else is gone, and to be singing in his own utopia of the songs. "You have to wonder if Johnson was playing for an audience that only he could see, one far off in the future," Dylan wrote in 2004 of the man who put "Come On in My Kitchen" into the world. He too could be singing to an audience only he could see, one far off in the past. With, sitting in chairs on the front porch of some general store, the likes of Robert Johnson, Lead Belly, Woody Guthrie, waiting to see if he had anything to show them.

* * *

It's April 1961 and Bob Dylan is in the kitchen of Gerde's. "I heard a voice coming cool through the screen of the radio speaker. Ricky Nelson was singing his new song, 'Travelin' Man'"—his girl-in-every-port song. "I had been a big fan of Ricky's and still liked him," Dylan would write in the first pages of *Chronicles,* "but that type of music was on its way out." Nelson was a huge star. "Travelin' Man" was his thirteenth record in the Top 10 since he debuted with a version of Fats Domino's "I'm Walking," the first of four Top 10 hits in 1957. He would reach the Top 10 only six more times after "Travelin' Man," and not once between 1963 and 1972 (with his version of Dylan's "She Belongs to Me" struggling into the Top 40 in 1969 and his "I Shall Be Released" falling short of the Top 100 a year later), when with "Garden Party," which was about a 1971 rock 'n' roll revival package show that Nelson played and Dylan attended, he came briefly back into the national story; he had only one more chart entry, the barely noticed "Palace Guard" in 1973. He died at forty-five in a plane crash while on tour in 1985. As Dylan called him up in *Chronicles* he was beginning a kind of dream of folk music that over the course of the book would set down the most vivid portrait there is of the call of a strange and foreign music—foreign because as a version of the American subconscious, a cauldron of all of its guilt and desire, it could seem more American than you were, more American than any other version of the country you'd ever stepped into. Nelson kept singing about his sweet fraulein down in Berlin town, but "It had no chance of meaning anything," Dylan said flatly. "It was a mistake. What was not a mistake was the ghost of Billy Lyon, rootin' the mountain down, standing 'round in East Cairo, Black Betty bam de lam. That was no mistake. That's the stuff that was happening. That's the stuff that could make you question what you'd always accepted."

* * *

That was the key: songs that cut the floorboards out from under your home, your school, broke up the concrete beneath your feet or your wheels, that gave you the burden and the freedom to invent the world you wanted to live in. It was, he said, "a parallel universe": a time and a place, Greenwich Village in the first years of the Kennedy administration, where the New Frontier was the old frontier, where "what was swinging, topical and up to date for me was stuff like the *Titanic* sinking, the Galveston flood, John Henry driving steel, John Hardy shooting a man on the West Virginia line . . . Folk songs were the underground story. If someone were to ask what's going on, 'Mr. Garfield's been shot down, laid down. Nothing you can do.' Nobody needed to ask who Mr. Garfield was, they just nodded, they just knew. It was what the country was talking about"—and how did Todd Haynes resist staging that conversation in front of a mock-up of the Waverly Diner on Sixth Avenue a block from Washington Square Park? That little all-night joint where folk singers hung out as the site of a culture not of taxicabs rushing up the broad street in waves and the subway station right outside the door but of a "culture with outlaw women, super thugs, demon lovers and gospel truths . . . streets and valleys, rich peaty swamps, with landowners and oilmen, Stagger Lees, Pretty Pollys and John Henrys—an invisible world that towered overhead with walls of gleaming corridors. It was all there and it was clear—ideal and God-fearing—but you had to go find it. It didn't come served on a paper plate. Folk music was a reality of a more brilliant dimension. It exceeded all human understanding, and if it called out to you, you could disappear and be sucked into it."

It was a myth, a story told around a secret campfire in hushed tones, lest the secret get out, and it was day after day. "There was a constant round of parties, jam sessions, song swapping, and hootenannies," Dave Van Ronk said of the place and time—and really, why hasn't anyone tracked down the woman people somewhere must have called Hootin' Annie? "The interest was obsessive, to the point that for a while there, except for my political friends, I did not associate with anyone who was not involved in folk music in one way or another." "The people I knew," Dylan said in 2001, "the people who were like-minded as myself—were trying to be folk musicians. That's *all* they wanted to be, that's *all* the aspirations they had. There wasn't anything monetary about it. There was no money in folk music. It was a way of life." But no matter how drunk anyone got, who was sleeping with who, who had a record coming out, who had the dope, who was paying the rent, whose couch you were camping on, something that could not only lead you to question what you'd always accepted but lead you to forget it was always nearby. Writing in 1960 in *Little Sandy Review* of late 1930s and early 1940s recordings made by John and Ruby Lomax of such indomitable and, until Alan Lomax recorded them again in the late 1950s, altogether forgotten performers as Vera Hall, from Alabama, in "Down on Me" and, with her cousin Dock Reed, "Motherless Children See a Hard Time," her voice, alone, without guitar or banjo or harmonica or even a stick to dress it, Jon Pankake confessed to an illusion that he was patently unable to completely abandon even as he saw through it. "Those of us who have known and studied with loving fascination these voices," he said of the original recordings, "veiled until now in a thick, 20-year-coating of surface scratch—for so long have, unconsciously I think, made them into legends in our mind's eye; have tended to mentally and emotionally place them in a never-never land of beautiful people and song where time was lost when the Lomaxes packed up their ancient disc recorder in the long ago." It was a fantasy, Pankake knew. As he wrote he knew Vera Hall's own words, her testimony, from 1948: "They don't hate us quite as bad, looks like, as they used to when I was a child. I seen the time you talk to a white person like my people do now, they'd kill you. But now when they walk up to your door, these old policy mens, these people tryin to sell you something, you can say any kind of impudent word to um . . . And you can push him out the door and they don't never be no more to it. But I seen the time, when I was a child, if you did anything like that, Lord, you just ready for all your family to be murdered. That's the reason I say it's better now, but it's still not yet over."

But it was precisely that never-never land, something, that as certain of the early sixties folk singers gathered it up, you can, as you listen to recordings now much farther away in time than the span Pankake was tracing, feel coming to life in your own heart. And you can hear it in the way Bob Dylan sang "When First Unto This Country" in 1989, off one of those hooted stages, thirty years after he first listened to Mike Seeger sing it, on one of the 1959 Newport Folk Festival albums on Vanguard.

When you listen to the most singular of the early sixties folk singers, you can picture a coven of monks, the protectors of knowledge in an age of pestilence and ignorance, having come down from their warrens in the hills to say what they know to those few who might listen. As an idea, as a fundamental value, that seems to be inside Dave Van Ronk saying "I did not associate with anyone who was not involved with folk music," of Bob Dylan saying "It was a way of life." You can't hear it in Van Ronk's records, though; you can't hear it in Pete Seeger, Oscar Brand, Leon Bibb, in the self-hallowed Kentucky singer Jean Ritchie, whose family was so steeped in the old music, she said, it was her very forebears who brought the likes of "Nottamun Town" to America, and so she owned it: not only morally, but the copyright. You can't hear it in the voices of so many others who took the stage at Newport in 1959 and the years after.

They don't have that monkish authority, that penitent's sense of mission. But you can hear it, in the next two or three years, in Joan Baez, Anne Briggs, Karen Dalton, and Bob Dylan. Not always, or even most of the time. It wasn't a spirit that was easy to catch, or to keep when you did. But it was there. On Baez's first album, from 1960, there was the British ballad "John Riley," probably from the 1600s if not before. It's about a testament of faith, and Baez sings it quietly, with an almost inhuman acceptance of fate—and in the circles she makes with the melody on her guitar, as what she wants plays wordlessly under the words declaring that she will give it up, the voice you hear plays less like that of a woman waiting for her lover across the sea than that of the pagan idol that set the story in motion. It's an acting out of a world in perfect balance—or a language that can be spoken only within the unwalled folk monastery.

"I was beginning to feel like a character from within these songs," Dylan wrote in *Chronicles* of learning "When a Man's in Love" and other traditional songs in Minneapolis, "even beginning to think like one." You can't listen to Anne Briggs and imagine her differently. She had dark hair, darker eyes—again, for all her beauty, there was something not simply human about her. In 1962, at seventeen, in Nottingham, she joined Ewan MacColl's Section 42, a traveling folk-music combine from London meant to spark people's culture in the hinterlands—she ran off to join the circus. She sang the oldest ballads, unaccompanied, like Vera Hall, as people had done hundreds of years before, her voice stilled in the air, breathless—as if she wasn't breathing, but letting the old songs breathe through her, as if she was daring to let anyone listening breathe, to break the spell. "I was a bit of a cuckoo in the nest," she said much later. "My heroes were the nameless people who were recorded in the field. Their singing, their songs were recorded, but rarely their names. But the singing struck a deep chord within me and I immediately felt 'that's my music, that's what I should be singing.' I didn't know it was called folk music, I just heard it and it was mine."

Her story is just as fablelike, just as too pure to be true.

She lived in poverty and squats, slept in the woods, disappeared for weeks to live alone on an island ("I do enjoy
people," she once said, "but I can live without them"),
drank herself into oblivion and then stood up to sing, fell
down, stood up again, climbed scaffolding and leaped
off, dove into canals at night like a witch. "All these songs
about roses growing out of people's brains and lovers
who are really geese and swans who turn into angels," as
Dylan said of folk music in 1966—this woman, who could
sound like a fantasy held in the tiny brain of the cuckoo
she sang about, who "sucks the little bird's eggs, to keep
her voice clear," was acting out that line as she herself
sang. "Willie O' Winsbury" is an ancient ballad about a
king who suspects his daughter has "been sleeping with a
man." He makes her strip naked, "That I may know you by
your shape, if you be a maiden or none." He decrees death
to the man who has taken her virtue—and when Willie is
brought before him, he is all but struck dumb:

> "And it is no wonder," said the king
> "That my daughter's love you did win
> For if I was a woman, as I am a man
> My bedfellow you would have been"

To hear Briggs move through those lines is to glimpse
a shape-shifting, to be caught, for a few moments, in a
dream of the uncanny, where reality slides through walls
of fact and leaves the dreamer shaking, awake with a ter-
ror that no matter how impossible, this happened, that it

can be forgotten but never erased. You want to play the song again; you're afraid to, afraid of what might happen if you do. "My memories are of her singing informally in pubs," said Éamonn O'Doughty, who in the 1960s worked in traditional Irish music. "You'd arrive in these country pubs with these bullock-like men standing around not taking very much interest in life and maybe after a pint or two and a bit of conversation Anne would launch into something and it would transform the moment, transform existence, transform everybody's life and probably the way they looked at their history."

Karen Dalton, in her music, may have taken this sense of folk music as its own world, as a negation of the ordinary, the predictable, of the life one was meant to live, the farthest. She was born in Texas in 1937 and grew up in Oklahoma; divorced twice by seventeen, with an abandoned child behind her, she was on the scene in Greenwich Village, singing jazz and blues. The albums she made, in 1969 and 1971, long after her time had passed and time had passed her by, didn't live up to the stories people told about her. Like so many folk singers, she was an alcoholic, then a drug addict; she died of AIDS in 1993 at fifty-five. In 1975, she sang on the Holy Modal Rounders' *Alleged in Their Own Time,* an album that included "Sally in the Alley," an obituary in advance by Peter Stampfel and his wife, Antonia Stampfel, bitter and disgusted. A sawing fiddle came up; Peter Stampfel's scratchy old-timey voice, as if from a 1920s Gid Tanner and his Skillet Lickers 78 with grooves worn through, came down.

Sally in the alley sifting garbage
Sally in the alley sifting junk
Sally in the alley sifting garbage
Sally in bed with a blue-eyed punk

Sally in the alley sifting garbage
Sally in the alley sifting shit
Sally in the alley sifting garbage
Sally in bed without a hit*

The only recordings that catch what was distinctive about her, that document how far she could go, appeared only in 2020, twenty-seven years after her death, on an album called *Cotton Eyed Joe:* tapes from performances at

---

* In August 2020, in an obituary on the website Perfect Sound Forever for his Holy Modal Rounders cofounder Steve Weber, Stampfel described the recording session with Dalton ("She knew about sally in the alley," he said in 2021): "Antonia and I had been taking fucktons of speed and doing music with Karen Dalton since late 1969, and she was going to do harmonies on two songs. Unlike Antonia and I, who drank speed mixed with fruit juice or soda pop, Karen insisted on shooting up, and 'had' to do so before doing any music. So off she went to the bathroom to do so while the rest of us, all set up to record, waited in the studio. And waited. And waited some more. Finally, I went to see what was holding Karen up. She was having trouble hitting a vein. She asked me to bring Weber, the Miles Davis of the needle. 'Karen can't find a vein and she needs you,' I told Weber. Off he stomped, muttering loudly about that damned Karen . . . they had been an on again/off again item. True to form, he hit her first try. Then Karen had brief convulsions, grabbed the bathroom sink, and ripped it completely out of the wall. That seemed to settle her down. She marched back to the studio and laid down a perfect harmony."

the Attic, a basement coffeehouse in Boulder, Colorado, in 1962. She was living with her young daughter in a shack in the mountains, in a five-person name-on-the-map called Copper Rock, where outhouses were amenities and water came from a stream. You can take that fact, then listen to her singing "Katie Cruel" to the fifty people that might be in the Attic, and believe that was all she could afford and all she wanted to, so that she could step back into a fantasy of the life lived by the first people to sing the songs she was singing. In a 1965 Public Television film called *Music Makers of the Blue Ridge,* Bascom Lamar Lunsford, whose 1920s records of "Little Moses" and "I Wish I Was a Mole in the Ground" appeared on Harry Smith's collection, is eighty-three. He's taking the young New York filmmaker David Hoffman on a tour through Madison County and Buncombe County in North Carolina, in the mountains near Asheville, introducing him to the best singers, dancers, players in his territory, and then his tone changes. They're going to Wilkes County, where Tom Dooley killed Laura Foster, to see Jesse Ray, "Lost John." They go up the hill. "Have I ever been here?" Lunsford's wife asks. "No," he says, as if now they're entering forbidden territory, "you've never been here with me." They arrive at a shack all but collapsed into a hillside. Lost John looks his name: a moon face, very few teeth, his skin appearing as if the top layer has been peeled off—he and his wife were brother and sister, as their parents were. In a checked shirt, a hat on his head, his fiddle held to his chest, he plays with his eyes closed, a beatific smile across his face. He rips out pieces of the melody, of the rhythm, forcing the few people listening, playing around him on banjo and guitar and autoharp, to jump across "Little Maggie" as if it were a rushing creek, just to hear him—what he's doing is too fast, and too rich, in the instant, with the music shooting past gravity, to hear all at once. There's a cut in the film, the melody shifts, and the music suddenly at once darkens and lifts so high all sense of reality falls away: this can't be happening. The idea of folk music breaks up: this is what is too good. You don't believe that two hundred years of music-making in these North Carolina hills could account for what this man is doing, or that two hundred years could take it away from him and give it back to a folk—and you don't believe it could have happened anywhere else. Dalton could sometimes conjure up the same paradox.

The uncanny creeps back. "She was not a college student singing folk songs," the one-time Attic manager Joe Loop writes in his notes to that 2020 album, "she was like the blues singers the students were emulating and she was the embodiment of the people the folklorists were studying"—and you can imagine that was both her life as it formed around her and a role she wanted to play.

"And I never saw her again," says one person after another in a 2021 film about Dalton, from all across Dalton's life. Her music was full of nihilism. She presented a sense of life where nothing has any value, but where songs might just barely carry at least a hint of the idea of value, because they can give a fading apprehension of shape, structure, everything that in everyday life was only an illusion. A song might pass on the feeling that once, somewhere, someone thought it was worth making, even if it was no longer possible to understand why that might have been, and make you wonder why it might be that the song hasn't disappeared. At their best the Boulder performances of mostly commonplace songs are the opposite of definitive. They're subjective, but the subjective individual singing—Who is she? What does she want? Where has she been?—is erased. Part of this is Dalton's playing—her guitar or banjo is just weather, scattershot, barely holding a rhythm for the stumbles she seems to want more. It's enough to get the song across—but the almost random nature of the music also opens the songs up. It passes them on, without leaving a mark to suggest that she ever played them, as they were passed on to her by whoever it was she's tried to forget. "Cook's place names were tools of traveling rather than fruits of travel," the poet and historian Paul Carter wrote of Captain James Cook's mapmaking following his landing south of what he would call Botany Bay in 1770, as the leader of the first Europeans to reach the eastern shore of Australia. "Rather than iron out the coast, reducing its otherness to a placeless classification, Cook's names served to preserve the space of exploring, to spread the coast out . . . Their function was to preserve the means by which they came to be known, the occasion of places, the sense in which places are means, not of settling, but of traveling on." That is the sense of art as in the Attic Dalton sings the likes of "Cotton Eyed Joe," "Mole in the

Ground," "Red Are the Flowers," "Pallet on Your Floor," "Darlin' Corey," "Pastures of Plenty."

"Pastures of Plenty" was always a curse of a song. In Woody Guthrie's original it was flat, a statement of facts about migrant labor, where his most self-consciously poetic line, "We come with the dust and we go with the wind" didn't sound poetic at all. For Dave Van Ronk it was a plea, all pain: *Can you see me? Can you hear me?* But Dalton's performance, her voice dry, acrid under that, feels as if she's remembering when the land went down to insects and drought and her family had to pack up and leave for that place in California that they heard was good for people like them, for Gilroy or San Jose, and since then life has played out as a variation of that scene again and again. It's the song of someone who has given up, someone who, as Lou Reed declaimed with pride in "Heroin," has decided to nullify her life, and singing this celebrated folk-world standard this way is part of making that happen.

She sings a song Vera Hall sang—though Dalton likely would have learned it from Lead Belly—sings it unaccompanied, as they sang it. "From West Texas," she says to the audience. "It's called 'Go Down, Old Hannah.'" And the singer addresses herself, as Old Hannah, and sings, 'Why don't you go down, and don't get up anymore.'" She sends it out as a song where life cheats the singer out of the death she wants and deserves.

Why don't you go down, Hannah
mmmmmmm-hmmmmm-mmmm-hmmmm

207

Don't you rise no more
Why don't you go down, Hannah
Don't you rise no more

"Nobody Knows You When You're Down and Out" was
written in 1923 by a vaudeville performer named Jimmie
Cox, just two years before he died at forty-two. It had
already been recorded by different people before Bessie
Smith took it up in 1929, and after that—after the way she
hummed herself through the last verse, as if to really tell
the story words were worthless—it was a song everyone
knew. Dalton takes it away from its shape as a jazz song—
with her it's a dirt song. It could not be more convincing—
it makes you feel as if most other times you've heard the
song were vanities. Now you are living the life of the character in the song as she describes it. You can see people
walking out of the little Boulder basement as quietly as
they can so they won't have to look the singer in the eye
when the song is finished.

She calls up the character that Barbara Loden wrote
and played in *Wanda,* her one movie as a director, in 1970,
about a woman in her thirties who trades her family for
the right to abandon it, as if what's left of her life will be
a quest to find out how much more can be given up. She
becomes a Little Maggie, someone who'll sleep with anyone for a drink. When she ends up in some cheap pres-
ent-day Bonnie-and-Clyde knock-off—not a knock-off
of the movie, from three years before, but of the fable,
as something as coded into the national imagination as

"When First Unto This Country," in its way as much a folk song as anything you could sing—it's with a man she meets when he's robbing a bar, and when he goes down in the bank robbery he's planned, with her as the lookout, she doesn't look back, and as you look into her eyes you see she isn't looking forward either. What the film critic David Thomson says about *Wanda* could be what anyone could say of Dalton's music: "It is a film that has no faith in story saving us, in the redemption of character, or the mercy of 'entertainment.' It is a film that adheres helplessly to a persistent state of alienation, aloneness, and absence of meaning." What is so striking about those words is the notion that a work of art could so obtain its own agency, could so follow its own mind, that it, not its supposed creator, someone called Barbara Loden, decides what it is and where it will go. You hear that in Karen Dalton's songs as she was singing them in 1962—as if she's just a vehicle, a carrier, an occasion in the life of the song, the monk inscribing the book and not signing his name. Or maybe from the same Dark Ages it's something more than that, the plague all around, the singer making music for flagellants.

"It meant nothing to me to rattle off things like 'Columbus Stockade,' 'Pastures of Plenty,' 'Brother in Korea' and 'If I Lose, Let Me Lose,' all back-to-back just like it was one long song," Dylan wrote in 2004 of starting out in New York. "Most of the other performers tried to put themselves across, rather than the song, but I didn't care about doing that. With me, it was all about putting the song across." But what if the song wasn't ready to come across? In his first year in New York, on July 29, 1961, at Riverside Church in Manhattan, Bob Dylan took part in an all-day hootenanny. One of the songs he sang was the English ballad "Handsome Molly," and it sounded exactly like the other old folk songs he sang that day. Every song was buried in the same illiterate-country-boy affectations. He wasn't singing songs, he was performing repertoire, proving there were songs he knew. If you listen today you hear a singer checking himself in the mirror of the audience, listening to himself, not the song—not listening for what the song can tell him. But at the Gaslight in the fall of 1962 everything has changed. Bob Dylan has changed; he can disappear into a song. That is what he went to the crossroads to get.

"I wish I was in London, or some other seaport town / I'd put my foot on a steamboat, and sail the ocean 'round," he begins, as if he's starting off as his own version of Ricky Nelson's "Travelin' Man." But a rushing hush from his guitar that seems to emanate from the music like wind puts an end to that. "My China doll down in old Hong Kong"—that wasn't real, and no one was supposed to think or even feel that it was. But in an instant, in the cloud of the song, Molly and the character in the song who's telling the story come to life as real persons. The drama between them is inescapable, even as the details in the words evaporate, pulled down by the overwhelming sense of loss that shapes the song. A confident, almost jaunty first step into a line is immediately brought down by the fact that the singer can never have what he wants, and by the fact that while he will think of Molly for the rest of his life, she will never think of him. If she ever did—if this isn't a story taking place all in his imagination, a man standing at the edge of a gathering, looking in, thinking of the life he should have had. "In reality/She doesn't even know me," as the Temptations would sing, so softly, because the words shame the singer. "You gave me your right hand," Dylan sings. "You said if ever you marry, I would be your man, but you broke your promise"—as the lines sway, the more you are swept away by the passion of the singer, the less you believe those words were ever spoken, the more you believe Molly and the singer have never even met. Still, her face is before him, he can imagine the promise she might have made, but he is so carried off by his own story that it generates its own verisimilitude. He hears her promise, he gazes on her face: "I could tell her mind was changing, by the roving of her eye." You're on the journey with him, around the world if that's what it takes to forget. And you follow Molly as she rides off, knowing how little he has to offer her, how fully the world is open to her as it's closed to him.

Just as Bob Dylan's true audience may be those who came before him, those he's trying not to dishonor when he sings their songs or makes those songs into new ones, it may be that his true biography is his inhabiting of other lives, whether they're musically inherited, like Handsome Molly, or coming to life in his own hands, the Franken-stein monsters, made of parts from different graves, the characters in his own songs, from Georgia Sam to the Rovin' Gambler to the fifth daughter on the twelfth night. That may be what was taking place when in 1993 he took up "Jim Jones."

*   *   *

The year before, on the day Bill Clinton was elected president of the United States, Dylan released *Good as I Been to You,* a self-produced, essentially homemade folk-guitar-and-harmonica album collecting the likes of the songs he'd been sneaking into his shows, named from one of them: "You're gonna quit me, baby/Good as I been to you." There were songs that at least formally belonged to others: versions of the Mississippi Sheiks' 1930 "Sittin' on Top of the World," Stephen Foster's 1854 "Hard Times." But most were floating songs with no known authors. As Constance Rourke said of minstrel songs, "many hands had been at work upon them": "Little Maggie," "Froggie Went A-Courtin'." There were folk-history songs, among them "Arthur McBride" and "Jim Jones," eighteenth- and nineteenth-century tales of, depending on how you heard them, innocents setting out on long journeys and the terrible betrayals they find when they reach their destinations, or imperialist class war and primitive capitalist exploitation, and as with "Handsome Molly" thirty years before they took on faces, Dylan inhabiting the first-person narratives as if he'd lived them twice. By this time in his career, in his life, these songs were Dylan's as much as anyone's. "Those old songs are my lexicon and my prayer book," he said in 1997, on the release of *Time Out of Mind,* an album where scores of fragments of the old songs were retrieved, rethought, rewritten, resung, until they made one new and whole long song. "All my beliefs come out of those old songs, literally, anything from 'Let Me Rest on That Peaceful Mountain' to 'Keep on the Sunny Side.' You can find my philosophy in those old songs."

He'd play some of the songs from *Good as I Been to You* over the next year or two, but the one he homed in on was the Australian prisoner's ballad "Jim Jones." It has been dated to the early mid-1800s—in the most common, standard version of the song, and Dylan's, the singer speaks of joining Jack Donohue, a leader of escaped convicts who was killed in 1830. But it feels much older—and in spirit the voice you hear could be coming from a veteran of the storied First Fleet, when in 1788 more than a thousand British prisoners were brought from Portsmouth to Botany Bay, to begin the history of Australia as a penal colony. In less than a week, with French ships now crowding the bay and little fresh water on shore, the whole enterprise moved north, to what is now Sydney—Botany Bay became a place to escape *to*—but in fable, that first site remained in the historical imagination as the worst place on earth. "The 'convict' who comes down to us in the pages of his oppressors," Paul Carter writes in *The Road to Botany Bay: An Exploration of Landscape and History,* on how the diaries, poems, and songs of the new Australians, the imprisoned Australians, were written out of the historical record, "is a social and political construction: he exists as a reflection of body of rules, as a personification of transgression, a figure of speech necessary to the ruling class's self-justification and the perpetuation of its power. To let the convicts speak for themselves would have been to entertain the unthinkable: mutiny, another history."

Come and listen for a moment, lads
And hear me tell my tale
How across the sea from England
I was condemned to sail
Now the jury found me guilty
Then says the judge, says he
"Oh, for life, Jim Jones, I'm sending you
Across the stormy sea
But take a tip before you ship
To join the iron gang
Don't get too gay in Botany Bay
Or else you'll surely hang
Or else you'll surely hang," says he
"And after that Jim Jones
It's high above on the gallows tree
The crows will pick your bones"

And our ship was high upon the sea
When pirates came along
But the soldiers on our convict ship
Were full five hundred strong

For they opened fire and somehow drove
That pirate ship away
But I'd rather have joined that pirate ship
Than gone to Botany Bay
With the storms ragin' round us
And the winds a-blowin' gale
I'd rather have drowned in misery
Than gone to New South Wales
There's no time for mischief there they say
Remember that, says they
Or they'll flog the poaching out of you
Down there in Botany Bay

Now it's day and night and the irons clang
And like poor galley slaves
We toil and toil, and when we die
Must fill dishonored graves
And it's by and by I'll slip my chains
Well, into the bush I'll go
And I'll join the bravest rankers there
Jack Donohue and co
And some dark night, when everything
Is silent in the town
I'll shoot those tyrants one and all
I'll gun the floggers down
Oh, I'll give the land a little shock
Remember what I say
They'll yet regret they've sent Jim Jones
In chains to Botany Bay

If you listen as you read, you can feel the song rocking back and forth, like a ship on a swell—that melodic rhythm is built right into the song, and the song may even have begun with that rhythm making a pattern in one person's mind, someone who then set out to find words for the cadence he or she was trying to follow. On *Good As I Been to You,* that is precisely how Bob Dylan plays it: his guitar is like two guitars, like the two guitars in Peter, Paul & Mary's "Don't Think Twice, It's Alright"; he surfs on the melody, bounces on it, the words too just part of the melody. That attraction may be why he spent nearly a year of his life on the song, rather than, say, "Sittin' on Top of the World," with as distinctive a tune and far more acolytes, from Big Bill Broonzy to Charley Patton to Robert Johnson to Howlin' Wolf to Cream and on down from there. But in 1993, from his first show of the year, in Dublin on February 3, to his last, in New York on November 17, he played "Jim Jones" thirty-one times, and since then he has never played it in public again. If a folk song has a thousand faces and you have to meet them all, in that year he enacted a small drama in which he set out to realize that charge.

At first that might not have been true at all. The song could have just come up as a placeholder in the set, with Bucky Baxter on steel guitar, John Jackson on electric guitar, Tony Garnier on bass, Winston Watson on drums, and Dylan playing acoustic guitar. For the first three shows, Dublin, London two days later and the next night, it's a ragged mess. The singing is strained and bleating. There's no timing, no rhythm, no melody. The song has no body. There isn't a true moment—except at the very end, on the second night, a high note, as if someone has glimpsed something in the music even if he can't find it. And then the next day, on February 9, still in London, it's all there. Though in the previous nights the song could drag on for nearly seven minutes, here it's barely five, yet it seems to move more slowly—and that's because for the first time there is a sense of a story being told, of something present to unfold. The melody is the front of the music, drawing the song out, now not eliding but pulling out the words, as if the singer doesn't want to tell this tale but can't resist the siren in his own song. For the first time Dylan takes a solo, comfortable with the song, interested in it, wondering where it will take him.

Over following shows new accents appear. There might be a drift in the drums, making the song into a dream. A Hawaiian sound from the steel guitar. A vehement vocal—angry, outraged, the story moving forward on its own disbelief. You begin to become familiar with the characters—the judge, the pirates, the sailors, the soldiers, the condemned. Or maybe it's that that's what's happening with the people who are playing the song. By the time they reach Louisville, Kentucky, on April 4, the bass and drums are gone: "There are no drums in a Bill Monroe band," Dylan said in 2015. "Hank Williams didn't use them either. Sometimes the beat takes the mystery out of the rhythm. Maybe all the time." There's something so satisfying about the melody—the way it seems to play the song with its own agency. It's all understatement, not letting the singer press any claims as far as he or she might want, so that it feels as if the melody repeatedly suspends every strand of the narrative, or any moral question at the end of a line. You can't wait for the next movement, for that creamy resolution, but at the same time you'd like to stay in the arms of what you've just heard, because it seems impossible that the next movement won't fall short, even if you've played the performance half a dozen times and know it won't. There's a rave-up almost six minutes in, a flurry of excitement, that seems to rise of its own accord. It ends at almost eight minutes with knife-strokes on Dylan's guitar, slashing at the song. People in the crowd are quiet at the end, as if they know they've been somewhere, and aren't yet back. In a review of Little Brother Montgomery's *Blues* in *Little Sandy Review* in 1961, Tony Glover quotes the singer: "There's a right way to play music—and there's a wrong way. You can't just play the way you feel . . . You have to know and study the tradition . . . The music has to come from within, yes, but you have to play it right." That could be the template for what Dylan is doing with "Jim Jones"—trying to find the right way to play it. And then the next right way.

Because two nights later in Nashville everything has changed. Dylan carefully counts off the melody, the meter, every indication of progression: he's dramatizing the start of the journey, all on his own guitar. It's displacing; you don't know where you are. Everything is suspended; he's actually not letting the story start. The guitar is tuned high, there are screams from the crowd, he quiets them. The suspense is awful. What's going to happen, in the song, in the hall? Are you sure you want to know? *Don't open that door*—all in the first minute. The band plays softly, easing into the music, no noise from the audience. The whole ensemble seems to pause over certain notes, letting the story live in memory as they pass over them, one moment to the next. Dylan's guitar in the last minute is reflective, elegiac—Jim Jones has been dead for two hundred years, and the feeling is that what happened to him could happen to anyone.

Over two shows in Virginia and Tennessee the song gets away from the band. In Asheville Dylan is back in the cave of the song, reading the scratches on the walls, the signs Jim Jones made in the cave where he hid before he was caught. Alone, Dylan plays into the song for a full minute before singing the first word, he plays solos once, then twice, twice as long as the first time, singing a verse, playing a verse, until for almost the last two minutes the song turns into something it hasn't come near to being before, a toe-tapper. It's all Dylan, investigating the song through the strings on his guitar. It's not smooth. There are slips. But the quest—the voyage Jim Jones describes, the will to run right out of it, is relentless and victorious. Did Weill and Brecht know "Jim Jones" when they wrote "Pirate Jenny"? As you listen to the echoes from Asheville it seems impossible that they didn't.

And so the song does take on different faces. Weary,

defeated, inflamed, living off fantasies of revenge, telling tales of who you'd kill and how you'd do it, counting the days of your sentence as you measure out the cadence of the song, and finally not counting, because the calendar was not your master: "When William Bryant made his successful escape in 1791," Paul Carter writes, "his term as a convict had all but expired. In escaping as a free man he was, in a sense, denying that Botany Bay had ever existed for him." In Beersheba, in Israel, on June 19, a face the singer hasn't seen before takes over, demanding an entrancing, disturbingly intimate vocal, and it sets the scene. "Hear me tell my tale"—in a crowded room, in a bar, you find the man next to you leaning over, whispering in your ear, his arm touching your shoulder. He's drunk, you want to move away, but you have the feeling that one tiny move and his hands would be on your throat.

And at the Supper Club in New York, for the last show of the year, the last time Bob Dylan sang "Jim Jones," they pick up the pace. Faster, urgent, a rock 'n' roll song, this could be "Outlaw Blues" from *Bringing It All Back Home,* "Don't ask me nothin' about nothin', I just might tell you the truth," it could be Gene Vincent's "Race with the Devil," Carl Perkins's "Blue Suede Shoes," the Primitives' "Crash"—this Jim Jones has broken out of jail. In the singing there is nothing to prove, no need to tell anyone anything, the world is just music, pieces of rhythm to jump over. The band is on it, with a big, grand sound. Farther into the song it's turned the corner into "Highway 61 Revisited," that fast, all stops out, the song looking over its shoulder and then driving off the shoulder of the road because it's not looking where it's going, as if Bob Dylan has decided he'll never play the song again—that there'll be no need to. The crowd is completely there—it erupts when the band guns into a break. Drums come up, the beat is commanding—they head into a curve, speeding up, louder, and Dylan is roaring. He never sang even "Like a Rolling Stone" with more delight and triumph. The audience is screaming for this hoary old folk song, and at all the right places, and the band is responding in time, everyone is now playing or shouting to the internal rhythm of the song, the history it will not resolve. Everyone is trying to give the song what it wants.

* * *

To take up the songs he put on *Good As I Been to You,* and again the next year, with *World Gone Wrong,* going deeper into old blues, gospel stories, twisting ballads, "Jack-a-Roe," "Stack A Lee," "Love Henry," "Delia," "Lone Pilgrim," Bob Dylan was, in one sense, performing as sincere and loving a tribute to Mike Seeger as anyone could. At the same time he was staking his claim to the tradition Mike Seeger and others had opened up for him. He was taking his place in the line of characters that inhabited the songs—as singers, and as the characters themselves. And yet he was also acting out a fatal paradox. "Seeger's adherence to a standard higher than himself could not be more evident," Robert Cantwell wrote in 1996. "What complicates the picture is that while he rescues in folk music the values dear to his class, values that typically include contempt for modern commonplaces such as mass production and mass culture, Seeger is also, through that music, in lifelong revolt against his class—and hence permanently exiled." One night in 1994, in his house in Lexington, Virginia, Mike Seeger talked about that state of exile, bitterly and in despair. What he had always wanted, he said, was not only to preserve and pass on what, as far back as 1904, the writer Emma Bell Miles, an educated woman who in revolt against her class turned her back on literate civilization and married a mountain man, called, in a historic *Harper's* essay, "Some Real American Music." He meant to take his place, alongside the likes of Dock Boggs, Clarence Ashley, John Hurt, his spiritual ancestors and contemporaries, as someone who had made his own unique contribution to the tradition they embodied, to be recognized as someone who deserved a place in that line. He might have followed the true vine, but as a well-born person, born in New York, he had been excluded from the brotherhood and sisterhood of the tradition itself—by scholars, folklorists, performers, even people who bought his records. *He* was a scholar—how could he be what he studied? Dock Boggs might have taken the stand for him in this court, but he was dead. And that meant, within the confines of his small, well-built house at the end of a narrow road, in the woods, with pictures of grandparents who went back to the Civil War on his walls, he would always in some ineradicable sense be homeless. I can still see his face as he talked. He was a warm, open, skeptical person, but his eyes were like two curses on himself.

And there was, cruelly, a deeper truth to what Mike Seeger was saying than could be defined by any question of class or origin. Compared with his one-time student Bob Dylan, there was a certain colorlessness in his voice, an inability to bring out those thousand faces. It was that engine of empathy. Because his sense of identification with other people, real, fictional, alive, dead, was greater, Dylan was able to get more out of the songs than Mike Seeger could. He could take them to places where they hadn't been before—and where he hadn't been before. If he couldn't play them as right as Mike Seeger could, he could play them better—with, in his own way, as much respect for the tradition, but with more of himself to give the tradition, to add to it.

As he sang "Jim Jones" across 1993, it was as if all the years of his great fame, from the time when he first abandoned the old songs and then played only his own, had been an apprenticeship. With his own recognition that the decades following the 1960s had led to dead ends, he finally settled into a state of being where he could take up the old songs again, and sing them as if he had written them himself and had been written by them, and he could even pass that on to people in his audience. He was now part of the tradition. It was his as much as anyone's. He could do whatever he wanted with it, including nothing. That true vine—he could take it or leave it. Almost thirty years after his long sojourn with Jim Jones he did that. He took it and left it, left it and took it. In the most expansive way, in a fractured, haunted, joking manner, where the only history that counted was the history traced in songs, in the midst of a terrifying global pandemic and an equally frightening election year, when no music was played in public, when in New York as later in São Paulo and New Delhi there was no space to put the dead, he put out a seventeen-minute single.

MURDER MOST FOUL

2020

Since the day it was released, every few weeks I find myself playing "Murder Most Foul." I can never play it less than three times in a row. Since Bob Dylan put the song on his website and saw it spread everywhere across the internet even before March 27, 2020, turned to March 28, it seems to bear more weight every time. The opening lines—"It was a dark day in Dallas, November '63 . . ."—still feel pumped up and fake, as if they were Vincent Price reciting "The Raven." But it's only an instant later that you realize, and it can be a shock every time, that you're listening in to John F. Kennedy's brain after the president-for-five-more-seconds has first been hit but before he's killed, arguing with his assassins as if there's still time to talk them out of it. "I saw some of myself in him," Bob Dylan said of Lee Harvey Oswald on December 13, 1963, at a dinner held by the Emergency Civil Liberties Committee at the Americana Hotel in New York, accepting its annual Tom Paine Award: "I saw things that he felt, in me."* He was booed

---

* Dylan later sent a long letter/poem to the committee, offering to

and hissed. It was that gift, or compulsion, of empathy, for those before him taken many steps too far. With "Murder Most Foul," Dylan exchanged roles, putting on Kennedy's bloody suit, coming back from that first bullet with the reply of the entitled, shuffled into the speech of any cowboy ballad, that "Wait a minute boys, do you know who I am?" and that voice, that argument, going on all through the song, all across its endless minutes which always seem to stop short—as the singer calls to Wolfman Jack, dead since 1995, to "Play that 'Only the Good Die Young,'" to hear "St. James Infirmary," "Tom Dooley," "I'd Rather Go Blind," "Blue Sky," "Cry Me a River," "Down in the Boondocks," "One Night of Sin," "Deep in a Dream," "Key to the Highway," "Dumbarton's Drums," with Kennedy's conversation with providence still going on, isn't there more for that DJ in the sky to play on his hydrogen jukebox? What about "Waterloo Sunset"? What about "Forty Miles of Bad Road"? *You do play requests, don't you, and who said I had to get off the line, just write it down, play "Key to the Highway" and "Anything Goes." Play Big Bill Broonzy's "Just a Dream," that "Dreamed I was in the White House, sittin' in the president's chair / I dreamed he's shakin' my hand, and he said, 'Bill, I'm so glad you're here,'" play Lou Reed, play "I dreamed*

___

return the award and not apologizing: "I am sick / so sick / at hearin 'we all share the blame' for every church bombing, gun battle, mine disaster, poverty explosion, and president killing that comes about. It is so easy t say 'we' and bow our heads together / I must say 'I' alone and bow my head alone . . . if there's violence in the times then / there must be violence in me / I am not a perfect mute."

I was the president of these United States / I dreamed I replaced ignorance, stupidity, and hate / I dreamed the perfect union and a perfect law, undenied / And most of all I dreamed I forgot the day John Kennedy died," you've got that one, don't you? We're just getting started, we're going to go all night. Wolfman Jack as the monk of the world of the song, holed up in his monastery of XERB Radio just over the Mexican border, taunting the FCC with his 250,000 watts of power, with the only copy of every song "Murder Most Foul" wants to play.

And though in the song Kennedy never stops that argument with fate, his voice maybe beginning to fade out at the end, perhaps halfway through the song the second time it ceases to be about the assassination at all. It seems more like drafts of two different songs picked up off the floor and woven together, or a cross between the Bible and *Where's Waldo?* All the seemingly obligatory lines, "The soul of a nation been torn away," fade into the film-noir dialogue that revs the song into the race away from Dealey Plaza it's describing, the oh-why-oh-why of "What is the truth, and where did it go" running straight into "Ask Oswald and Ruby, they oughta know" ("I can do a few other people's voices," Dylan said in 1978. "Richard Widmark. Sidney Greenstreet. Peter Lorre"). The song lifts off into Hieronymus Bosch's *Apocalypse,* his *Garden of Earthly Delights,* but with Bosch not painting but singing it. Eden, earth, hell—it becomes a sermon, Dylan rolling through some Mickey Spillane exegesis of a particularly resistant passage in Revelation in the Sinatra-alone-at-the-bar-in-his-trench-coat-and-hat-while-the-party-swirls-around-

him-on-the-cover-of-*No-One-Cares* voice of the albums
that cleared the way for "Murder Most Foul," Dylan sounding weathered, beaten down, but interested, watching
the piano player in the mirror behind the bar, thinking
of Hoagy Carmichael fingering the keys in Uncle Butch's
in *The Best Years of Our Lives* as in the studio Fiona Apple,
Alan Pasqua, and Benmont Tench do the same.* This is
his stroll through "The Night We Called It a Day," "Once
Upon a Time," and "These Foolish Things" on *Shadows in
the Night* in 2015, *Fallen Angels* in 2016, the triple-album
Triplicate the year after that, fifty-two songs from "I'm a
Fool to Want You" to "Why Was I Born." "This particular
record is how he sounds right now," Elvis Costello said of
"Murder Most Foul," "informed by the seven years that he
sang standards. That's long enough to become a priest."

In 1968, in an interview in *Sing Out!* with John Cohen
and Happy Traum, Bob Dylan explained "Murder Most
Foul." "The thing about the ballad," he said,

> is that you have to be conscious of the width of it at all
> times, in order to write one. You could take a true story,
> write it up as a ballad, or you can write it up in three
> verses. The difference would be, what are you singing

---

* "They were playing a demo. I heard it and I just couldn't believe
it," Pasqua said of the recording session for "Murder Most Foul." "In rock
music, things usually have a specific beat and pulse. This was free. It was
elastic. It wasn't specific to a certain time or tempo. It just flowed. When I
was done listening to the track, I turned to Bob and I said, 'My god, Bob, this
sounds to me like *A Love Supreme*.' He just stopped and he looked at me."

it for, what is it to be used for. The uses of a ballad have changed to such a degree. When they were singing years ago, it would be as entertainment . . . a fellow could sit down and sing a song for a half hour, and everybody could listen, and you could form opinions. You'd be waiting to see how it ended, what happened to this person or that person. It would be like going to a movie. But now we have movies, so why does someone want to sit around for a half hour listening to a ballad? Unless the story was of such a nature that you couldn't find it in a movie. And after you heard it, it would have to be good enough so that you could sing it again tomorrow night, and people would be listening to hear the story again. It's because you want to hear that story, not because you want to check out the singer's pants. Because they would have that conscious knowledge of how the story felt and they would be part of that feeling . . . like they would want to feel it again.

"Everybody could listen, and you could form opinions": in many ways the true story of the song, when it had barely begun to live its life, before it had begun to make its way into the world, was in the noise around it. "Rock 'n' roll forms its own society," Dylan once said, echoing Emily Dickinson: "The Soul selects her own Society"—here it's as if a single song has done that, done both. The explosion of have-you-heards. The what-do-you-thinks, from all over the world, from people you might never imagine wanting to talk about a Bob Dylan song. It was recorded in

February 2020, when the shadow of disease was hanging over the world but before the country shut down, before Joe Biden knew he would have the chance to become the next president and not, perhaps, the last to run—but it felt like the world had been waiting for this since 1963 without knowing it, even people not born in 1963 had been waiting for it since 1963, with 1963 not merely a date but an idea. It was a friend saying, "You want to play it over and over. It's so beautiful. But this is death, this is about now, this is about the virus—he thinks he's going to die. Think of how he lives—in an airplane all the time, smoking. This could be the last Bob Dylan song. And I wonder what Stevie Nicks thinks of being in there—almost everyone else he names is dead." From an editor in Cambridge: "Comes over me like a fever. Seems to tell the story about how evil swept over the nation til now when we have succumbed to the most foul murder of the soul of our nation." "It's a good song to argue about," as a film director from Paris was doing—"I read the incredibly stupid piece the New Yorker published on Dylan's amazing new track which has been giving me chills in my back from start to finish"—as a film critic from San Francisco was asking, "I have just endured half of Dylan's new song about JFK. Did he have to do this?" Again there was Elvis Costello, apparently not hurt that he wasn't on the playlist: "Where he sings that litany of names, song titles, and films—that actually brought me to tears. Just the fact that there was the consequence of all that piled up, and the coincidence and then the jokes within it, where some of the names don't seem to be in the same standing as some of the others, so they're said with a little aside. It wasn't pious. It wasn't grandiose. It's all piled up for you to view. What I don't understand is saying it's about JFK. It's a bit like saying *Moby-Dick* is about a whale. You know, it sort of is, nominally, but it's not really, is it?"

Within a day, the first cover version appeared on You-Tube. Within a month, there was an epic parody, a set of lyrics nearly twice as long as the original, "Last Thoughts on Bob Dylan's Homebound Covid Blues," where Dylan was addressed as the DJ and all the songs were his, from "Masters of War" to "I Contain Multitudes." There was the score of people writing in to the *Guardian* in London to answer back to its pompous formal review ("a testament to his eternal greatness") with their own opinions formed while listening to the ballad, among them one Jubby Tayor: "His songwriting is like a billboard with 50 years of layers." There was Charles Pierce in *Esquire* on March 30, stunned, shocked, and lucid to the bone: "It is a walk down the full length of desolation row." There was Peggy Noonan in the *Wall Street Journal,* saying nothing that memorable sentence by sentence, but capturing the act of listening to the song in her tone of voice, a sense of respect and luck, for having shared times. And there were, instantly, the hundreds of definitive Captain Midnight Decoder Ring analyses of every word tying the entirety of the performance down to its last syllable to a specific online JFK conspiracy lecture, with quotes from the song about sliding down a banister and Gerry and the Pacemakers' 1964 "Ferry Cross the Mersey" deciphered as references to the Jim Garrison assassination suspects Guy Banister and David Ferrie—if not to the Masonic conspiracy, with a citation from the song about watching the Zapruder film thirty-three times signifying the magic inherent in the number three in Masonic lore (though, maybe because it was just too obvious, the author neglected to mention that in 1965, in an interview with *Disc Weekly,* Dylan claimed to have thirty-three guitars). Each piece was completely convincing and dedicated to the proposition that there is a one-dimensional explanation for anything—as, if explanation is what you're looking for, there almost has to be.

It was a final contradiction of what "Murder Most Foul" is, and how it plays. Again it comes back to empathy, that ability to listen to other people, people one met in songs, people one met in life. "I wish, that for just one time, you could stand inside my shoes," Bob Dylan once sang, setting up the most devastating close in any of his songs. "And just for that one moment"—and here an emphasis came down, hard and final: "And just for that one moment, I could be you." "I saw all the characters in this song and elected to cast my fortunes with them," he wrote in *Chronicles* of "Dignity," from 1994, written after he heard that the basketball player Pete Maravich had died at forty, in words that apply to everyone named in "Murder Most Foul."

That one-dimensional form of discourse of the village explainer dissolved when people began to play with the song, creating their own versions, as if it really were an old ballad that everybody knew. On the air on April 9 was Gideon Coe's BBC "Murder Most Foul Themed Special"—

or, as he put it after playing the song and setting up to play every song mentioned in the song in three hours, "Bob Dylan Bingo." He didn't make it, because he didn't play snippets, he didn't make a chart. He went from singer to singer, style to style, the line "Play John Lee Hooker" coming out as more than ten minutes of Hooker and Canned Heat not even beginning to exhaust the possibilities of "Boogie Chillen." "Mystery Train" never sounded so much like a miracle, and newsbreaks on the spread of the pandemic ("The prime minister has been moved out of intensive care") created the feeling of people calling out to each other from their graves as the show went on: with just these two songs, Bill Black, 1926–1965, Alan "Blind Owl" Wilson, 1943–1970, Elvis Presley, 1935–1977, Bob "The Bear" Hite, 1943–1981, Henry "Sunflower" Vestine, 1944–1997, John Lee Hooker, 1917–2001, Scotty Moore, 1931–2016, Larry "The Mole" Taylor, 1942–2019. And there were the videos, at first simply layering literal illustrations over every name or place in the song, but then beginning to reimagine the song, as if it had no copyright. There was one that replaced the music on the record, led by Fiona Apple's first piano, with a loop of John Lennon's piano on "Imagine," the music so lulling, so similar to the cocktail jazz Alan Pasqua had composed as background music for Dylan's Nobel Prize lecture, that it took me seven or eight minutes to catch on. There was one that slowed the twenty-six-and-sixth-tenths seconds of the Zapruder film so that it ran for seventeen relentless minutes as the song played over it. There was the Hollywood editor Bob Mori's untrammeled re-creation, where Dylan's description of the assassination as the "Greatest magic trick under the sun" materialized as footage of Houdini beginning his strait-jacket performance, tied up and raised in front of an office building with PINKERTON DETECTIVE AGENCY painted on the windows, as if they'd be on the case as soon as Houdini was loose, and where the line "Blackface singer, white-face clown" was suddenly the not-quite-explicably-right sequence in Max Fleischer's 1933 production *Betty Boop in Snow White* where Koko the Clown loses his clothes and changes into a rubber-legged contortionist ghost, the whole production ending at that seventeen-minute finish line with unbearable footage from John F. Kennedy's inaugural address: "If a free society cannot help the many who are poor, it cannot save the few who are rich."

This was all a testament to the first fact of the song: the strange way that it can hardly be heard once without sparking anyone's need to hear it again—a world gathering around a campfire of unanswerable questions, and it takes everyone around the campfire to hear the whole song.

* * *

When "Murder Most Foul" sounds its final notes, under "Play 'The Blood-Stained Banner,' play 'Murder Most Foul,'" like a gong more in the way Dylan says the words than in the way the musicians play their last notes, it can feel like far more than a song is ending. Is that why the song forces you to play it again, so that you can put that ending at bay? So it, whatever that might be—life, the story life tells, the day, leaving you nothing left to do and nothing you can think about—won't end? All of the year ahead was in the song, the hundreds of thousands dead, some of whom, like the producer Hal Willner, who staged a concert for Bob Dylan's birthday in 2018 in New York at Town Hall, and who died of Covid-19 on April 7, 2020, eleven days after "Murder Most Foul" appeared, got to hear it. "He made it sound like America," a friend said of Dylan's lovely performance of the accursed "Once Upon a Time" that closed the special *Tony Bennett Celebrates 90* in 2016, as Dylan swayed back and forth holding the microphone stand, as if caught in wind no one else could feel—and in the way that "Murder Most Foul" with its American playlist not only sounds like America but feels as if it means to take it in, to account for it, this passage from the last issue of *Little Sandy Review,* signed, as for so long almost none of their work had been, by Jon Pankake and Paul Nelson, which Bob Dylan would have read, and maybe thought about, sounds to me like "Murder Most Foul."

It was a review of the Carter Family's *'Mid the Green Fields of Virginia,* a collection of work from the 1920s and '30s: "Certainly the Carter Family intuitively understood and magnificently expressed in their songs what has taken the sociologists and historians decades of thought to discover: that we are a nation of outcasts from Western civilization, doomed to forever devour and plunder the land we cannot cherish, to dream of fathers and kings and to love guiltily in the night. The hopeful falsehoods of our 'official' art pale before the nightmare of our folk art, though it speaks its truths in absurd sentimentality to balm with self-pitying tears the pain of direct confrontation. Like the Carter Family longing for the green fields of home, we may share these songs of lost innocence, but neither the sharing nor the innocence is the essential experience we seek. It is, rather, the longing itself." And there is, there, an echo of Pankake's ruminations over the descent of Vera Hall and others from their recordings in the thirties to the inescapably faded recordings they made twenty years later: "The more sentimental of us," he wrote, with words that were really cold-blooded and hard-boiled, "have difficulty facing the knowledge that when these singers are gone, they shall have taken a part of America with them, and their kind will never be seen on the face of the earth again."

There is film, from the 1964 Newport Folk Festival, of an interview with Mississippi John Hurt, who first recorded in 1928, who was found by blues mavens who sent him a letter addressed only by his name and "Old Blues Singer" to Avalon, Mississippi, because of his 78 "Avalon Blues," and who now, in his seventies, was making new LPs. "There are only two reasons not to buy this record," I remember a friend saying of Hurt's 1966 album *Today!* "Either you can't afford it, or you're stupid." His old records had appeared on Harry Smith's *Anthology of American Folk Music;* that was what the interviewer was asking about. "You didn't think of it as folk music at the time, did you?" the interviewer asks. "Well," Hurt says, "I didn't know what folk music was—I began to kind of learn what they meant by folk music . . . I think it means songs that . . . what I call 'em, died out. Went back and renew 'em. That right?" It's somewhere backstage; in a confluence too perfect to believe, as John Hurt speaks, you can hear Bob Dylan singing "Mr. Tambourine Man" to the crowd. "The Bible says the old men teach the younger ones," Hurt says finally. "I'm glad I've got something they want."

"He wasn't there to see the last of the traditional people," Bob Dylan said some years ago, when a writer suggested an affinity between him and a younger singer. "But I was." He was speaking of John Hurt, and others of Hurt's time who were part of the folk world in the 1960s. Dock Boggs. Skip James. Sara and Maybelle Carter. Bascom Lamar Lunsford. Clarence Ashley, who once sat on a Newport stage fidgeting half to death as Bob Dylan sang "Only a Pawn in Their Game" in front of him. Even, perhaps, Mike Seeger. He meant that he saw what went out of the world with them. What will go out of the world with him?

NOTES

Quotations not otherwise identified are from Bob Dylan.

Epigraph: Nat Hentoff, "The Crackin', Shakin', Breakin' Sounds," *New Yorker,* October 24, 1964.

FREQUENTLY CITED

Bob Dylan: The Essential Interviews. Jonathan Cott, ed. Wenner Books, 2006. Cited as Cott.

Cantwell, Robert. *When We Were Good: The Folk Revival.* Harvard University Press, 1996. As Cantwell.

Carter, Paul. *The Road to Botany Bay: An Exploration of Landscape and History.* Knopf, 1988. As Carter.

Dylan, Bob. *Chronicles: Volume One.* Simon and Schuster, 2004. As *Chronicles.*

———. "MusiCares 2015 Person of the Year Address." *Rolling Stone,* February 9, 2015. As MusiCares.

Dylan on Dylan: Interviews and Encounters. Jeff Burger, ed. Chicago Review Press, 2018. As Burger.

No Direction Home: Bob Dylan. Directed by Martin Scorsese. *American Masters*/PBS, 2005. As Scorsese.

Rotolo, Suze. *A Freewheelin' Time: A Memoir of Greenwich Village in the Sixties.* Broadway, 2008. As Rotolo.

Scaduto, Anthony. *The Dylan Tapes: Friends, Players, & Lovers Talkin' Early Bob Dylan,* interview transcripts edited by Stephanie Trudeau. University of Minnesota Press, 2022. As Scaduto.

Shelton, Robert. *No Direction Home: The Life and Music of Bob Dylan* (1986). 2nd ed., Backbeat, 2011. As Shelton.

Sounes, Howard. *Down the Highway: The Life of Bob Dylan* (2001). 2nd ed., Grove, 2011. As Sounes.

BIOGRAPHY

"He had taken off": Sounes, p. 214. Brackets in original.
"Vanished without a word": Barack Obama, *A Promised Land* (Crown, 2020), p. 543.

IN OTHER LIVES

"I can see myself in others": "Press Conference, Rome, 23 July 2001," Burger, p. 413.
"I once wrote a song": Nat Hentoff, "The Crackin', Shakin', Breakin' Sounds," *New Yorker,* October 24, 1964, Cott, p. 16.
"Writing a song": "Izzy Young's Notebook, 20 October 1961–14 March 1962," *The Fiddler Now Upspoke* (U.K., n.d.), Burger, p. 8.
"Someone who's telling me": Cameron Crowe, liner notes to Dylan, *Biograph* (Columbia Records, 1985), p. 38.
"I've been married": "Interview with Edna Gunderson," *USA Today,* September 11, 2001, Burger, p. 435.

BLOWIN' IN THE WIND / 1962

"I knew it was bull": Shelton, p. 52.
"The moment of real poetry": "All the King's Men," *International Situationniste 8,* January 1963, *Situationist International Anthology,* edited and translated by Ken Knabb (Bureau of Public Secrets, 1981), p. 116.
"The words you've just read": Bob Dylan, *Blowin' in the Wind* (Sterling, 2012).
"It's meant to underscore": Jeff Rosen, "Forrest Gump," email received by GM, January 18, 2021.
"Flat-top Gibson": "Interview with Ron Rosenbaum," *Playboy,* March 1978, Burger, p. 204. The giving-up-the-electric-guitar story is told in different versions, set in different times and places. This is simply the earliest time and place citation I have found.

"Jesus Christ": "Interview with Bruce Helman," KMEX, Tucson, Arizona, December 7, 1979, Cott, p. 272.

"I want to tell you a story 'bout it": Recording provided by Parker Fishel of Bob Dylan Music.

"He had an uncanny ability": Rotolo, p. 12.

"During that time": Rotolo, p. 103.

"Group acted as if": Bob Spitz, *Dylan: A Biography* (W. W. Norton, 1989), pp. 190–91.

"Folk music is wide open": "Izzy Young's Notebook, 20 October 1961–14 March 1962," *The Fiddler Now Upspoke* (U.K., n.d.), Burger, p. 7.

"I had a teacher": "The Last Word: Odetta," *New York Times,* December 4, 2008.

"I decided to leave": Edmund Wilson, "Greenwich Village in the Early Twenties, 'The Road to Greenwich Village,'" *The Shores of Light* (Farrar, Straus and Young, 1952), p. 81.

"I like the land": "Bob Dylan's First Recorded Interview, October 1961." Posted on YouTube, October 2, 2020. Billy James was the head publicist at Columbia Records, called in by the producer John Hammond before Dylan's first recording session "to write some promo stuff on me, personal stuff for a press release," Dylan later wrote. He began by telling James he was from Illinois and that his parents were "long gone." "Billy seemed unsure of me and that was just fine," Dylan went on. "I didn't feel like answering his questions anyway, didn't feel the need to explain anything to anybody," *Chronicles,* pp. 7–8.

"It was a whole community": "Interview with Kurt Loder," *Rolling Stone,* June 21, 1984, Cott, p. 295.

"Got out of the car": Scorsese.

"Sometimes we would make": Shelton, p. 73.

"Born in Duluth": "WNYC at 90: Bob Dylan's First Radio Interview." WNYC *New Sounds,* posted July 8, 2004. Bob Dylan, *From Minnesota to New York 1958–1961* (bootleg), as "Oscar Brand Folk Song Festival, WNYC Radio October 29th 1961," CD 4, track 16.

"Pete Seeger": Anthony Scaduto, *Bob Dylan: An Intimate Biography* (1971) (2nd ed., Signet, 1973), p. 69.

"A figure on the order": Joshua Clover, "Bob Dylan Writes 'Song to Woody,'" *A New Literary History of America,* ed. Greil Marcus and Werner Sollors (Harvard University Press, 2009), p. 906.

"I knew I was gonna": Christopher John Farley, "The Legend of Bob Dylan," *Time,* September 15, 2001, Burger, p. 436.

"You know the stories": Scorsese.

"Mr. Dylan is vague": Robert Shelton, "Bob Dylan—A Distinctive Folk-Song Stylist," *New York Times,* September 29, 1961, *Bob Dylan: A Retrospective,* ed. Craig McGregor (William Morrow, 1972), p. 18.

"He came in waving": Mikki Isaacson to Anthony Scaduto in a passage not used in his 1971 *Bob Dylan.* Scaduto, pp. 211–12.

"*Everybody* wanted that": Scorsese.

"Quietly, Bob said": Rotolo, p. 158.

"Just like Shakespeare": Christopher John Farley, "The Legend of Bob Dylan," *Time,* September 15, 2001, Burger, p. 436.

"Much time was spent": Rotolo, pp. 9–10.

"The folk industry": "Editors' Column," *Little Sandy Review,* no. 17, n.d., p. 45.

"If you sent your child": "LEON BIBB; TOL' MY CAPTAIN (Vanguard 9058)," "HARRY BELAFONTE: SWING DAT HAMMER (RCA Victor 2194)," *Little Sandy Review,* no. 2, n.d., p. 29. "I'm glad I'm too old for day camp," the folk singer Cynthia Gooding wrote in response eight issues later; *Little Sandy Review,* no. 10, n.d., p. 39.

"The nightmare of our folk art": Jon Pankake and Paul Nelson, "OLD-TIME SOUTHERN DANCE MUSIC (Old-Timey X-100)," "A COLLECTION OF MOUNTAIN FIDDLE MUSIC (COUNTY 501)," "THE CARTER FAMILY: 'MID THE GREEN FIELDS OF VIRGINIA (RCA Victor 2772)," *Little Sandy Review,* no. 30, 1965, p. 13.

"To find expression": "JOAN BAEZ (Vanguard 9078)," *Little Sandy Review,* no. 8, n.d., p. 13. The review was also an answer to the liner notes by Vanguard head Manny Solomon: " 'She does not follow those singers who painstakingly imitate the rich ethnic heritage, often thereby submerging their own personalities and more often draining the tradition of its essentially dynamic, creative qualities.' This approach to folk singing may be valid for an extraordinary bundle of talent like Joan Baez, but it is generally pretty deplorable to this reviewer, who happens to believe that to find expression . . . "

"This new class": "P-FOR-PROTEST," *Little Sandy Review,* no. 25, n.d., p. 9.

"I reckon some folks": "Quotable," *Little Sandy Review,* no. 6. n.d., p. 7.

"On our cover": "Editors' Column," *Little Sandy Review,* no. 11, n.d., p. 2.

"He set our brains jingling": Thomas Ruys Smith, "Dead Presidents:

'Charles Giteau,' 'White House Blues,' and the Histories of Smithville," *Harry Smith's* Anthology of Folk Music: *America Changed by Music,* ed. Ross Hair and Thomas Ruys Smith (Routledge, 2017), p. 186.

"Part of the folk police": *Chronicles,* p. 248.

"He took about twenty or thirty": Paul Nelson in Kevin Avery, *Everything Is an Afterthought: The Life and Writing of Paul Nelson* (Fantagraphics, 2011), p. 13.

"He popped up": "I Am My Words," *Newsweek,* November 4, 1963.

"Implying with relish": Rotolo, p. 253.

"*Newsweek* wanted to do a cover": to Anthony Scaduto in a passage not used in his 1971 *Bob Dylan.* Scaduto, pp. 243–44.

"There is even a rumor": "I Am My Words," *Newsweek,* November 4, 1963.

"We recall Bob": "BOB DYLAN (Columbia 1779)," *Little Sandy Review,* no. 22, n.d., pp. 13, 14. It was actually Sigma Alpha Mu.

"The new breed": "P-FOR-PROTEST," *Little Sandy Review,* no. 25, n.d., p. 9.

"That such a creative energy": "THE FREEWHEELIN' BOB DYLAN (Columbia 1986)," *Little Sandy Review,* no. 27, n.d., pp. 24, 25.

"The big question": "Editors' Column," *Little Sandy Review,* no. 28, n.d., pp. 42–43.

"Dig the latest": "Editors' Column," *Little Sandy Review,* no. 29, n.d., p. 4.

"June 1962": Bob Dylan, "Blowin' in the Wind," *Sing Out!* June 1963.

"When it was later discovered": David Mikkelson, "Blowin' in the Wind," snopes.com, May 3, 2014.

"Bob is not authentic": Matt Diehl, "It's a Joni Mitchell Concert, sans Joni," *Los Angeles Times,* April 22, 2010.

"Topical songs have been the topic": "WBAI Broadside Show, New York City—May 1962," collected on Bob Dylan, *Man on the Street* (Reel to Reel bootleg, disc 6).

"It was folk music": Rotolo, p. 218.

"He had the traditional attitude": Peter Stampfel, email received by GM, September 3, 2020.

"So here I am": James Williamson, "Last Night a Record Changed My Life," *Mojo,* July 2018.

"When you say": "Press Conference, Rome, 23 July 2001," Burger, p. 413.

"There are certain songs": "Interview with Ron Rosenbaum," *Playboy,* March 1978, Cott, p. 225.

"During the concert": Rotolo, pp. 255–56.

"If you sang": MusiCares.

"In the early 1960s": John Mackie, "Canada 150: Ian Tyson, the Cowboy Folksinger," *Vancouver Sun,* June 24. 2017.

"A thousand faces": *Chronicles,* p. 71.

"A few skeptics": Neil Hickey, "Bob Dylan: ' . . . A Sailing Ship to the Moon,'" *TV Guide,* September 11, 1976, Burger, p. 214.

"I really was never any more." *Chronicles,* pp. 116, 155, 121, 147, 148, 146.

"Dylan's eyes darted": Jim Miller, "Bob Dylan," "The Sixties," *Witness,* vol. II, no. 2–3, Summer–Fall 1988, pp. 53, 68. Part of a remarkable collection of essays including Casey Hayden's "The Movement," as affecting an attempt to rescue lost history as one will ever read.

"It's a beautiful song": Glen Cooper, "Bob Dylan: Live Aid Rehearsals," YouTube, June 2, 2020.

"An extension of what was going on": "Interview with Bill Flanagan," bobdylan.com, March 22, 2017.

"The supreme moment": Cantwell, p. 351.

"Looked like seminarians": Cantwell, pp. 351–52.

"How could he write": Scorsese.

"I grew up": Chris Kup, "From First-Year Students to Coach K, K-ville Protest Organized by Nolan Smith Draws a Crowd," *Duke Chronicle,* August 27, 2020.

"You can't do the same things": Noel King, "How a Mother Protects Her Black Teenage Son from the World," NPR, June 3, 2020.

THE LONESOME DEATH OF HATTIE CARROLL / 1964

"It is a no": Pauline Kael, "The Glamour of Delinquency," *I Lost It at the Movies* (Little, Brown, 1965), pp. 54, 40.

"If you don't like the news": Scoop Nisker, *If You Don't Like the News . . . Go Out and Make Some of Your Own,* self-released LP, 1970.

"Dropping out of a world": Sandy Darlington, "Cream at Winterland Playing to Overflow Crowds. 6000 of Us Each Night," *San Francisco Express-Times,* March 14, 1968, "Cream at Winterland" (edited version), *Rock and Roll Will Stand,* ed. Greil Marcus (Beacon, 1969), pp. 77–80.

"Most people living in the United States": Glenn Ellmers, "Conservatism Is No Longer Enough," *The American Mind: A Publication of the Claremont Institute,* March 24, 2021. The heading illustration was a photo of a hairy-armed white man binding his hands in readiness for a fight.

"I ran into Al Grossman": Theodore Bikel, "Interview for the Edelson Society," c. 2011–12, YouTube.

"The first time I heard the song": Christian Scott aTunde Adjuah, "80 Artists Pick Their Favorite Bob Dylan Song for Bob Dylan's 80th Birthday," ed. Ryan Leas, Stereogum.com, May 24, 2021.

"I wrote 'Hattie Carroll' ": Cameron Crowe, liner notes to Bob Dylan, *Biograph* (Columbia Records, 1985), p. 44.

"He's a no-account": Sounes, p. 147.

"You've got to have power": *Chronicles,* p. 219.

"One of the best songs": Paul Nelson, "IDOLS, IDOLS, IDOLS . . . " *Little Sandy Review,* no. 29, n.d., p. 15.

"A mixture of rage and severity": Paul Nelson, "Bob Dylan," *The Rolling Stone Illustrated History of Rock & Roll,* ed. Jim Miller (Rolling Stone/Random House, 1976), p. 213. Nelson, suffering from dementia, was found dead of starvation in his apartment in New York, having convinced himself, despite regular income from Social Security, that he had no money to buy food. He is a model for the lovingly drawn character Perkins Tooth in Jonathan Lethem's 2009 novel *Chronic City.*

" 'In the courtroom of honor' ": "Blood Ties," *Homicide,* NBC, October 17, 24, 31, 1997. Story by Tom Fontana, Julie Martin, and James Yoshumura. Written by Anya Epstein and David Simon. Directed by Mark Pellington. Jeffrey Wright played the killer.

"I told you 'The Times They Are A-Changin' ": Bob Dylan, *The Gospel Speeches* (Hanuman, 1990), pp. 12–13.

"It went through every sphere": conversation with Laurie Anderson, San Francisco, February 13, 2019.

AIN'T TALKIN' / 2006

"Producer said, 'Jack' ": Jack Scott, "The Way I Walk," Warren, Michigan, August 23, 2014, YouTube.

"I am I": D. H. Lawrence, *Studies in Classic American Literature* (1923) (Viking, 1964), p. 45.

It's a structure: Steven Rings, " 'What Did You Hear, My Blue-Eyed Son? Or, the Musical Sources of 'Hard Rain' (and why 'Lord Randal' Isn't Among Them)," "The World of Bob Dylan," University of Tulsa, May 30, 2019, unpublished, courtesy Steven Rings.

"I moved the dial up": *Chronicles,* pp. 32, 33.

"Every line": "Radio Interview with Studs Terkel, WFMT (Chicago), May 1963," Cott, p. 6.

"Someone pointed out": "Interview with Robert Hilburn, *Los Angeles Times,* April 4, 2004," Cott, p. 436.

"I was not an expert on Bob Dylan": Bryan Ferry, email received by GM, February 21, 2021; Ferry's "Hard Rain" reached number 10 in the U.K.

"I heard him sing": Dave Van Ronk, with Elijah Wald, *The Mayor of MacDougal Street* (Da Capo, 2005), p. 206.

"I'd walk into a bar": Bettye LaVette, with David Ritz, *A Woman Like Me* (Blue Rider, 2012), pp. 315–36.

"Once the evening has arrived": Niccolò Machiavelli, "Machiavelli's Letter to Fransceso Vettori of 10 December 1513," *Machiavelli and His Friends: Their Personal Correspondence,* ed. and trans. J. B. Atkinson and David Sices (Northern Illinois University Press, 2004), p. 264. Written from Machiavelli's farm in exile from Florence, the deepest exile: "I love my native city more than my own soul," he wrote again to Vettori fourteen years later.

"The whole history of these tales": Constance Rourke, *American Humor: A Study of the National Character* (1931) (New York Review, 2004), pp. 75, 76.

"Mastered by his own irony": Eric Lott, *Love and Theft: Blackface Minstrelsy and the American Working Class* (1993) (Oxford University Press, 2013), pp. 102, 103.

"Our negro slaves": James Kennard Jr., "Who Are Our National Poets?" *The Knickerbocker,* October 1845, *Selections from the Writings of James Kennard, Jr., With a Sketch of His Life and Character* (1848) (facsimile ed. University of California, Wentworth, 2019), pp. 107, 125, 114.

Kennard was born: "A Sketch of His Life and Character," *Selections from the Writings of James Kennard, Jr.* (Ticknor, 1849; facsimile edition University of California, 2007), pp. xxiii–xxiv.

"Old Dan Tucker was a fine old man": Frank Goodwyn, "Old Dan Tucker," recorded by John Lomax, Falfurrias, Texas, April 30, 1939, loc .gov/item/lomaxbib000138/.

"A combination of the lever": John Phoenix, "Tushmaker's Tooth Puller" (n.d., c. 1850s) feastofbooths.net, 2016. Also in 2016 the *Journal of the History of Dentistry* published " 'Tuskmaker's Tooth Puller':

The Beginning of Dentistry's Technological Revolution?" by Thomas P. Kroll, DDS, of the University of Texas.

"One of the feelings": Richard Avedon and Doon Arbus, *The Sixties* (Random House, 1999), p. 21.

THE TIMES THEY ARE A-CHANGIN' / 1964

"I sang a lot of 'come all you' songs": MusiCares.

"It was ironic": "Editors' Column," *Little Sandy Review,* no. 30, p. 4. In *Esquire,* Jerry Lewis was "BOMB OF THE YEAR" for his TV show, Dylan part of "THE ZORI SANDALS AWARD," which also went to Joan Baez, Peter, Paul & Mary, "and folksingers everywhere," with "whole-hearted editorial support from this publication for any foundation or institution whose aim it is to desophisticate the hillbilly."

"They're saying: 'Trump is our rightful president' ": Luke Broadwater, "Black Officer Felt Mob's Fury and Sting of Racism," *New York Times,* February 26, 2021, p. A17.

"In the mid-Sixties": Paul Nelson, "Bob Dylan," *The Rolling Stone Illustrated History of Rock & Roll,* ed. Jim Miller (Rolling Stone/Random House, 1976), p. 208.

DESOLATION ROW / 1965

"At the time": John Hammond to Anthony Scaduto in a passage not used in his 1971 *Bob Dylan.* Scaduto, pp. 235–36.

"I immediately differentiated": *Chronicles*, pp. 282, 284.

"It was on the western frontier": Margaret Vandergrift, "The Clown's Baby" (1890), dlyrics.com.

"Even if Desolation Row": Joshua Clover, email received by GM, August 7, 2021.

"Only by their size": "Questioning of Sandra Teale by a private investigator," Michael Fedo, *The Lynchings in Duluth* (1979) (Minnesota Historical Society Press, 2000), p. 180. "Sandra Teale" is a pseudonym for Irene Tusken.

"Wasn't so sure that the truth": *Chronicles,* 226.

"Yet, by 1992": William D. Green, Foreword to Michael Fedo, *The Lynchings in Duluth* (1979) (Minnesota Historical Society, 2000), p. vii.

JIM JONES / 1992

"Who looked like Ava Gardner": *Chronicles,* p. 62.

"Bon voyage": *Chronicles,* pp. 63–65.

"Tugboat captains": *Chronicles,* pp. 66–67.

"The best balladeer in the land": *Chronicles,* pp. 67–69.

"Folk music existed outside the corruption": William Hogeland, "American Dreamers," *Inventing American History* (Boston Review/MIT Press, 2009), p. 52.

"Leading the relatively sheltered lives": "THE FIRST ANNUAL UNIVERSITY OF CHICAGO FOLK FESTIVAL," *Little Sandy Review,* no. 12, n.d., pp. 5–6.

"Well, you're in Greenwich Village": *Lomax the Songhunter,* directed by Rogier Kappers (PBS, 2006).

"And so as I walked up": Maddie Deutch, lecture no. 13 in my course "The Old Weird America: Music as Democratic Speech—From the Commonplace Song to Bob Dylan," New School University, December 2, 2009.

"A face and figure": Cantwell, pp. 40, 41.

"He was extraordinary": *Chronicles,* pp. 69–70.

"By the fifth word": John Fahey, "The Center of Interest Will Not Hold," *How Bluegrass Music Destroyed My Life* (Drag City, 2000), p. 279. Fahey imagines himself at a last Hank Williams show on a riverboat on the Potomac in 1953: when he sang "Alone and Forsaken," Fahey says, "many of us almost died of grief and fright."

"Whatever the song called for": *Chronicles,* pp. 70–71.

"The thought occurred to me": *Chronicles,* p. 71.

"Folk music is the only music": Nora Ephron and Susan Edmiston, "Interview with Nora Ephron and Susan Edmiston. *Positively Tie Dream,* August 1965," Cott, p. 50.

"My mother and I": John Hiatt, "80 Artists Pick Their Favorite Bob Dylan Song for Bob Dylan's 80th Birthday," ed. Ryan Leas, Stereogum .com, May 24, 2021.

"The audience slowed their chattering": Rotolo, p. 11.

"You have to wonder": *Chronicles,* p. 285.

"I heard a voice": *Chronicles,* pp. 13–14.

"A parallel universe": *Chronicles,* pp. 14, 20, 103, 236.

"There was a constant round of parties": Dave Van Ronk, with Elijah Wald, *The Mayor of MacDougal Street* (Da Capo, 2005), p. 48.

"The people I knew": "Interview with Mikal Gilmore, *Rolling Stone,* 22 December 2001," Cott, p. 424.

"Those of us": Jon Pankake, "THE BLUES ROLL ON (Atlantic 1352)," *Little Sandy Review,* no. 10, n.d., p. 25.

"They don't hate us": "Nora—Gifted to Sing," Alan Lomax, *The Rainbow Sign: A Southern Documentary* (Duell, Sloan and Pierce, 1959), p. 109. Vera Hall's autobiography as told to Lomax, who renamed her "Nora" to protect her. Hall (1902–1964) was born and died in Alabama.

"I was beginning to feel": *Chronicles,* p. 240.

"I was a bit of a cuckoo in the nest": Colin Harper, "Anne Briggs," notes to *Anne Briggs: A Collection* (Topic, 1999).

"All these songs": "Interview with Nat Hentoff, *Playboy,* March 1966," Cott, p. 98.

"My memories": Colin Harper, "Anne Briggs," notes to *Anne Briggs: A Collection* (Topic, 1999).

"No, you've never been here": *Music Makers of the Blue Ridge,* directed by David Hoffman (Public Television, 1965); reissued as *Bluegrass Roots* (Hoffman Collection, 2010). All of Hoffman's Lost John footage, including a sequence where Lunsford stops to ask for directions and receives a set of instructions it would take a crow to decipher, can be found on YouTube as "Rough Old-Time Mountain Folk Make the Best Music."

"She was not a college student": Joe Loop, liner notes to Karen Dalton, *Cotton Eyed Joe: The Loop Tapes, Live in Boulder, 1962* (Megaphone, 2020).

"And I never saw her again": *Karen Dalton: In My Own Time,* directed by Richard Peet and Robert Yapkowitz (Greenwich Entertainment, 2021).

"Cook's place names": Carter, p. 32.

"It is a film that has no faith": David Thomson, *A Light in the Dark: A History of Movie Directors* (Knopf, 2021), p. 227.

"It meant nothing to me": *Chronicles,* p. 18.

"Many hands had been at work": Constance Rourke, *American Humor: A Study of the National Character* (1931) (New York Review, 2004), p. 76.

"Those old songs": "Interview with Jon Pareles, *New York Times,* 28 September 1997," Cott, p. 396.

"The 'convict' who comes down to us": Carter, p. 295.

"There are no drums": Robert Love, "Bob Dylan: The Uncut Interview," *AARP: The Magazine,* February–March 2015, Burger, p. 491.

"There's a right way": Tony Glover, "LITTLE BROTHER MONTGOMERY: BLUES" (Folkways 3527)," *Little Sandy Review,* no. 13, n.d., pp, 25–26.

"When William Bryant": Carter, p. 303.

"Seeger's adherence": Cantwell, p. 43.

MURDER MOST FOUL / 2020

"I saw some of myself": Address to Emergency Civil Liberties Committee, "Bob Dylan and the NECLC," corliss-lamont.org, includes Dylan's later letter to the committee.

"I can do a few other people's voices": "Interview with Ron Rosenbaum, *Playboy,* March 1978," Cott, p. 227.

"They were playing a demo": Ray Padgett, "Alan Pasqua Talks 'Murder Most Foul,'" *Flagging Down the Double E's,* March 2021.

"This particular record," Madison Bloom, "Elvis Costello on the Music of His Life," Pitchfork.com, November 30, 2020.

"The thing about the ballad": "Interview with John Cohen and Happy Traum, *Sing Out!* October/November 1968," Cott, p. 121.

"Rock 'n' roll forms its own society": "Interview with Ron Rosenbaum, *Playboy,* March 1978," Cott, 224.

"Where he sings that litany": Madison Bloom, "Elvis Costello on the Music of His Life," Pitchfork.com, November 30, 2020.

"A testament to his eternal greatness": Alex Petridis, "Bob Dylan: Rough and Rowdy Ways—a testament to his eternal greatness," *Guardian,* June 13, 2020.

"His songwriting is like a billboard": "A Billboard with Fifty Years of Layers: Readers on Bob Dylan's Rough and Rowdy Ways," ed. Ben Beaumont-Thomas, *Guardian,* June 24, 2020.

"It is a walk": Charles P. Pierce, "Last Call with Charles P. Pierce—It Was Indeed a Murder Most Foul," Esquire.com, March 30, 2020.

Peggy Noonan, "Bob Dylan, a Genius Among Us," *Wall Street Journal,* June 18, 2020.

"I saw all the characters": *Chronicles,* p. 169.

"Certainly the Carter Family": Jon Pankake and Paul Nelson, "OLD-

TIME SOUTHERN DANCE MUSIC (Old-Timey X-100)," "A COLLECTION OF
MOUNTAIN FIDDLE MUSIC (COUNTY 501)," "THE CARTER FAMILY: 'MID
THE GREEN FIELDS OF VIRGINIA (RCA Victor 2772)." *Little Sandy Review,*
no. 30, 1965, pp. 12–13.

"The more sentimental of us": Jon Pankake, "THE BLUES ROLL ON
(Atlantic 1352)," *Little Sandy Review,* no. 10, n.d., p. 25.

"You didn't think of it as folk music": *American Epic,* directed by
Bernard MacMahon (BBC/PBS, 2017). "John Hurt was the inspiration
for *American Masters,*" MacMahon said when I asked him whether Bob
Dylan playing while Hurt was speaking was real. He described going
through Newport footage for his own documentary—earlier in the film
we have seen Hurt tell the story of receiving his first 78 in the mail,
of taking it to the home of a white woman who had a phonograph,
and hearing it, as she played it, outdoors, through an open window,
because black people were not allowed in the house. "I was reviewing
a reel and I saw his beautiful face and thought, 'Wow, this looks like an
interview.' When we projected the film and he started talking, I heard
the unmistakable harmonica playing in the background. He must have
been behind the main stage. The hairs on the back of my neck stood
up." "I knew then," he said, "that I had the end of my film."

"He wasn't there": conversation with Dave Marsh, Newport Folk
Festival, August 3, 2001, courtesy Dave Marsh.

ACKNOWLEDGMENTS

My first thanks go to Jeff Rosen, who is not responsible for anything here, other than a single line of his own, but whose knowledge, crusty opinions, and deadpan manner have always been inspiring. Then to Joy Murphy and Mac Cimino of Universal Music. Then at Yale, for the counsel and enthusiasm of John Donatich, the constant responsiveness of and direction from Abbie Storch and Danielle D'Orlando, the painstaking work of freelance indexer Meridith Murray and proofreader Bob Land, and the great umbrella of the indefatigable Susan Laity. I thank the designer Dustin Kilgore, and for the cover, the artist Max Clarke of thumbnail. I was so lucky to work again with Dan Heaton, the so-called copyeditor who is really the bad conscience and good friend of every writer he works with, down to the most unforgivable error he catches and the impossible sentence he questions with a sardonic wave, each query a call to live up to his standards and his taste. My appreciation and respect for my agent Emily Forland of Brandt and Hochman, along with Marianne Merola and Henry Thayer, only grows with each book.

Acknowledgments

Many people helped me in many ways, including Kevin Reilly who in 1994 sent me three CDs collecting all of Bob Dylan's performances of "Jim Jones" in 1993, which I listened to many times over the years. For what it's worth, in some ways that is the real germ of this book.

I thank Emily Marcus, Laurie Anderson, Peter Stampfel, Parker Fishel, Clinton Heylin, Matt Jacobson, Doug Kroll, Larry Jenkins, Eric Lott, Cecily Marcus and Steve Perry for finding me a complete set of *Little Sandy Review,* Jon Pankake, Jeanie McLerie, Colleen Sheehy, Paul Metsa, Barbara Portnoy, Mark Davidson of the Archive of American Song in Tulsa, David Thomson, Lindsay Waters, Clive Priddle, Olivier Assayas, Bill Hogeland, Laura Cronk and Lori Lynn Turner of the Writing Program at New School University, Sean Wilentz, Maddie Deutch, Jenn Pelly, Steven Rings, Michael Goldberg, Barry O'Connell, Alexia Smith, Diego Siglio of PAC–Padiglione d'Arte Contemporanea, Milan, Joshua Clover, Sean Latham, and for a spark, Steven Zipperstein.

In the chapter on "Blowin' in the Wind," part of the commentary on "See That My Grave Is Kept Clean" draws on a talk I gave in Tulsa in 2019 at "The World of Bob Dylan" symposium, which was later published in *The World of Bob Dylan,* edited by Sean Latham. The chapter on "The Lonesome Death of Hattie Carroll" originally took shape, in much shorter form, as a talk for a conference on music and politics in Milan, scheduled for February 28, 2020, five days after the mayor shut down the city. I also draw on two paragraphs from "Old Songs in New Skins," a

Acknowledgments

column published in the April 1999 issue of *Interview* and collected in my 2010 anthology *Bob Dylan by Greil Marcus;* on "Silent Warnings," from the December 1981 issue of *California;* and on parts of two items in my column Real Life Rock Top 10, from the May 28, 2000, issue of *Salon* and the August 6, 2003, issue of *City Pages,* both collected in my 2015 anthology *Real Life Rock.* Here and there, if not quite everywhere, various paragraphs and sentences first appeared in different form in various of my Real Life Rock Top 10 columns.

"I think we're going to be listening to this for a long time," my wife said the first time we heard Bob Dylan's *John Wesley Harding,* playing from start to finish on KMPX on one of the first days of 1968. That album is not specifically in this book, because it's the air it breathes. What Jenny said is its motive and its touchstone.

CREDITS

INDEX

Songs, albums, and books not otherwise referenced are written, recorded, or sung by Bob Dylan. Names in parentheses following folksongs or spirituals not identified as "traditional" indicate the performer.

Index

"Ballad of Donald White, The," 54
"Ballad of Hollis Brown," 5, 71–72n, 162
Band Aid, 65
Bannister, Guy, 234
Baran, Roma, 107–8, 110
"Barbara Allen," 193
Baxter, Bucky, 216
Beach Boys, 134
Beckwith, Byron De La, 96
Bee Gees, 17
Belafonte, Harry, 35, 38, 180
Belvin, Jessie, 150n
Belzer, Richard, 66
Bennett, Tony, 8
Benton, Thomas Hart, 181
Berger, John, 66
Betty Boop in Snow White (film), 236
Bibb, Leon, 38, 199
Biden, Joe, 74, 232
Bielecki, Bob, 108
Bikel, Theodore, 95n, 99, 179
Bill Monroe and His Bluegrass Boys, 23
Black, Bill, 23, 235
Blake, Jacob, 80
Blanchett, Cate, 60
"Blind Willie McTell," 67
Blonde on Blonde, 44, 192
Blood on the Tracks, 192
"Blowin' in The Wind": Arnold, 50; Chad Mitchell Trio, 21–22; Cooke, 17; DeShannon, 17; Dietrich, 17; Dylan, 11–12, 14–24, 28–30, 46, 48–51, 54, 57, 59, 61–64, 69–71, 71–72n, 72–73, 75–78, 95, 192; Faithfull, 17; Millburnaires, 50–51; New World Singers, 22–23; Odetta, 16; Peter, Paul & Mary, 22, 51,

55, 57n, 71–72n, 99; Staple Singers, 27, Wright, 16
"Blue Moon of Kentucky": Bill Monroe and His Bluegrass Boys, 23; Elvis Presley, 23
"Blue Suede Shoes" (Perkins), 220
Blues (Little Brother Montgomery), 218
Bob Dylan (album), 41–42
"Bob Dylan's 115th Dream," 2, 48, 150
"Bob Dylan's Dream," 58–59
Boggs, Dock, 181, 183, 222, 239
Bon Jovi, Jon, 139
"Bonnie Lass o' Fyvie, The," 42
Bono, 65
Boomtown Rats, 65
"Boots of Spanish Leather," 162
Bowers, Pete, 182. *See also* Seeger, Pete
Brand, Oscar, 32, 199
Bridges, Lloyd, 173
Briggs, Anne, 199, 200–202
Bringing It All Back Home, 150, 220
Broadside, 21, 22, 46
Broadside Ballads, Vol. 1, 22
"Brother in Korea," 209
Brothers Four, 41, 51
Brown, Jim (as fictional character), 74
Bruce, Jack, 88
Buckingham, Lindsey, 117
Bud and Travis, 40
"Buddy Won't You Roll Down the Line" (traditional), 181
"Burning Bridges" (Scott), 123
Burroughs, William, 111
"But Beautiful," 153

Cannon's Jug Stompers, 180

262

Index

Index

Index

Index

Index

Index

Index

Index